Coping with Computers

Comparative Economic

COPING WITH COMPUTERS

A Manager's Guide to Controlling
Information Processing

Henry C. Lucas, Jr.

THE FREE PRESS
A Division of Macmillan Publishing Co., Inc.
NEW YORK

Collier Macmillan Publishers
LONDON

The Free Press
A Division of Macmillan Publishing Co., Inc.
866 Third Avenue, New York, N. Y. 10022

Collier Macmillan Canada, Inc.

Printed in the United States of America

printing number

1 2 3 4 5 6 7 8 9 10

Library of Congress Cataloging in Publication Data

Lucas, Henry C.
  Coping with computers.

  Includes index.
  1. Electronic data processing—Management. I. Title.
QA76.9.M3L83   1982   001.64′024658   82-71887
ISBN 0-02-919310-9

Text passages from pp. 78–79 and 362–364 of *The Analysis, Design, and Implementation of Information Systems,* 2 ed., by Henry C. Lucas, Jr., copyright © 1981, 1976 by McGraw-Hill, Inc., used [as edited] with the permission of McGraw-Hill Book Co.

Text passages from pp. 138–139, 184–185, 187–188, 281–282, 293, and 295–297 of *Information Systems Concepts for Management,* 2 ed., by Henry C. Lucas, Jr., copyright © 1982, 1978 by McGraw-Hill, Inc., used [as edited] with the permission of McGraw-Hill Book Co.

For Ellen,
Scott, and Jonathan

Contents

Preface

THIS BOOK IS INTENDED for senior-level managers and is designed
to help them understand their role in information processing. I
find managers in this position uneasy about information processing; they feel that it controls them rather than vice versa.

Senior managers have a crucial role to play in assuring successful systems. Because the technology is so pervasive, no area of
the firm will be left untouched by computing. The purpose of this
book is to help the manager gain a basic understanding of
computer-based information systems and their management.

The power of the technology seems incredible. Technology is
not the main issue, however; our problem is how to apply and
manage information processing. The management team and
organization able to cope with information processing will have a
competitive advantage over firms that continue to mismanage
computing.

I would like to acknowledge the help of all the managers who
have shared their problems and perspectives on computers with
me. McGraw-Hill has helped by allowing me to reproduce
material from two of my earlier texts. Much of this book was written while I was on a sabbatical leave at IBM's European Systems

Research Institute at La Hulpe, Belgium. I thank my colleagues there, who provided stimulating ideas and a superb environment for writing. In particular, I am indebted to John D'Arcy, Oliver Johnson, Chris Smit, and Pradeep Mathur.

I also wish to thank Ms. Carole Larson for her help with the manuscript. Finally, I owe a great deal to my wife, Ellen, who is one of the best managers I have ever encountered.

Coping with Computers

CHAPTER 1

Why Bother?

WHY SHOULD A MANAGER be interested in computing? I have heard this question in a variety of forms from students, managers, and users of systems. For those who hope that ignoring computers will make them go away, the news is bad: computers are here to stay. Future historians will call this period "the electronic revolution," a period whose advances overshadow the industrial revolution of the last century.

My objective in this book is to present ideas and concepts for managers who confront computers and information systems in their jobs. The treatment here is largely nontechnical, though there will be occasional references to technical issues. Based on more than 15 years of consulting and research on information systems, this book attempts to answer critical questions for managers. Even if the reader disagrees with the answers, I hope the discussion provides some insight into how to cope with computers and information systems.

The Role of Information Processing

It is easy to give one's own area of specialization an exaggerated importance in the firm. The financial executive sees finance as the

1

key to the business, faculty members feel that their own areas of research are the most crucial to the profession. While I firmly believe that information processing is critical to all that we do, it is true that most organizations are not going to flourish or even survive if all they do is process information. There are many facets to an organization, and it is almost impossible to say that any one of them is solely responsible for success. However, information is sufficiently critical that most organizations will not succeed or achieve their potential if they fail at information processing.

Individual Processing

We are all information processors both on and off the job. Figure 1–1 depicts the way in which people look at information. This view stresses the fact that information cannot be defined for someone else; information is the meaning given to data by the person who perceives it.

The nature of the problem influences the interpretation of data. The decision by an oil firm to enter a new line of business, the manufacture of electric motors, is far more important than the decision to lease additional office space. The consequences and the costs involved, plus the impact on the organization, mean that data will be scrutinized much more closely for this strategic move.

FIGURE 1-1   Influences on the Interaction and Use of Information

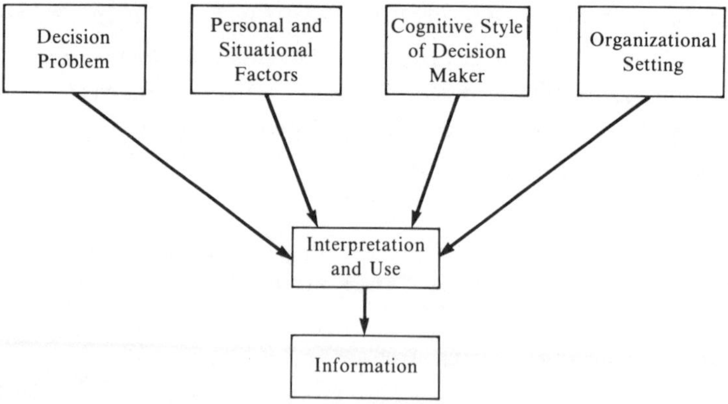

The situation of an individual influences his or her approach to information processing. As mentioned earlier, we have a tendency to view problems through our own specialties; I see information-processing problems when I look at a company, while my colleagues in marketing see a marketing problem. I observe the same data that they do, only I interpret it differently through my frame of reference.

An individual's decision-making style will influence the way data are processed. Some managers reason analytically, with numbers dominating their approach. Other managers reason more heuristically or intuitively; they are not interested in numbers. There is a large class of individuals who want little data for input into their decisions at all. Such an individual usually has his or her mind already made up, based on subjective criteria or hardened attitudes; we often refer to this class of people as "close minded."

Finally, the organizational setting affects the way we view problems. We tend to adopt or at least to be influenced by the attitudes and positions of those around us. After spending many years in an organization, we are socialized by it. It would not be surprising to find that an executive of an automobile firm may have an entirely opposite interpretation of data on pollution to that of a long-time member of the Sierra Club.

While all of these differences in the way data are interpreted present many problems in developing information systems, they should help motivate us to continue. Information processing is critical to everything that we do—what better reason to find out more about it? In particular, we need to examine the disasters that can result when computers, processing millions of pieces of data in a second, are programmed incorrectly or operate a poorly designed system.

Processing in Organizations

The president of a garment manufacturer wants to receive an accurate weekly report of bookings, shipments, and production by garment and by color. The chief executive of a major conglomerate spends several hours a day using a terminal to access key performance statistics. Financial institutions process millions of transactions each day worth billions of dollars, electronically.

There is one feature that almost all organizations have in common; they must acquire and analyze information. Figure 1-2 asks us to stretch our imaginations for a moment and to think of the organization as an entity that processes information. The firm collects data from a number of places, such as its own internal operations and customers. Most organizations also attempt to collect data on their competition and on other factors outside the firm. Government statistics as well as purchased data like stock prices, economic forecasts, and so forth are employed for this purpose.

The firm processes all of these data, sometimes employing a computer system for part of the analysis. Managers take some type of action based on this analysis, like beginning a new advertising campaign, removing a product from the market, merging with another firm, and so on. The action is monitored to find out what happens, and all of these data become feedback for further examination.

Why No One Seems to Care

While the foregoing discussion attempts to point out the critical importance of information processing, the question still occurs:

FIGURE 1-2   The Organization as an Information Processing Entity

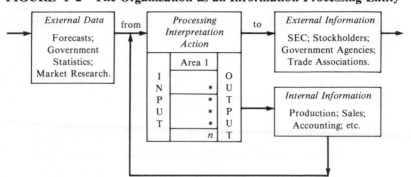

why do so few people outside the profession seem to want more knowledge about this phenomenon? My experience suggests some of the following reasons for the lack of enthusiasm among students and managers confronted with information systems.

1. *They have given up.* Because of frustrations, poor service, badly designed systems, computers that are hard to use and understand, the beleaguered user has simply decided that the computer age really isn't here yet; he or she will wait for something usable to appear.

2. *The technology is too intimidating.* I would venture that most managers know a great deal more about every other functional area than they do about information processing. Even if an individual has spent 20 years in accounting, that person still has learned quite a lot about his firm's marketing, sales, production, and finance functions. The lowest level of knowledge of most managers is about information processing. One likely reason for this sorry state of affairs is that the technology seems foreign and difficult to understand—something that is the fault of those of us in the computer profession.

3. *Key decisions seem to be based on technology instead of management considerations.* For the most part, managers have been asked to make decisions regarding computers based on changes in the technology, not on the business plan of the firm. New computers and major new programs have been authorized on the basis that new technology is available to process data on-line, to build a data base, or to distribute computing to users. One objective of this book is to help managers wrest control of information processing from the technology so they can control it, just as management controls other facets of the business.

4. *Lack of interesting computer use.* Many firms have specialized in rather mundane and uninteresting applications of computers. It is hard to consider something that is used as a high speed printing device or fast calculator as very exciting or worthy of much management attention. However, these computing devices have a great deal of potential if we can learn how to manage and apply them creatively.

5. *Lack of experience and education.* For many managers, the need to confront information-processing systems or computers

has never arisen. For these lucky few, there is no need to deal with the issues raised here, unless a system is likely to be developed soon. And that is the unfortunate part; as present trends continue, there will hardly be anyone left in the firm who is untouched by computing, especially at the management level. However, if one has not experienced information systems before, it is easy to remain unaware of the chaos created when one makes mistakes. One does not appreciate the ease with which errors are made and the vast number of things that can go wrong in the design and operation of computer-based systems.

The Shape of Applications

During my career in this field, I have been struck by the creative and exciting ways in which computers have been applied to a variety of situations. The following examples will illustrate some of these uses.

Market Research

A market research firm in the Midwest saw that point-of-sale systems were not being rapidly adopted by supermarkets. These systems feature automatic reading devices at the grocery checkout counter which scan the universal product code on the customer's purchases. The scanner is connected to a computer in the store that looks up the price of the item and adds it to the check. At the same time store inventory is reduced. At the end of the list of purchases, the program prints a total for the customer to pay.

The equipment vendor states that the advantages of such a system are faster checkout (which means that more individuals can be served in the same period of time) and better inventory control. Because of the high investment cost and objections by some consumer groups, stores have been slow to adopt the technology.

The market research firm picked two towns that had

demographic characteristics similar to the rest of the U.S. and offered to place the point-of-sale equipment in selected grocery
stores at no charge. The only condition was that the equipment
had to be connected to the market research firm's computer in
Chicago.

Once the equipment was installed, this firm had an extremely
valuable edge on their competition. It could conduct experiments
for clients and provide immediate, accurate results. As an example, suppose that a client wanted to introduce a new detergent.
The market research firm could design a series of experiments in
which certain areas of a city were exposed to radio advertisements,
another section to free samples, and a third to special store
displays. The results in terms of purchases can be monitored
directly in the stores and a report can be prepared for the client.

Project Control

My university has an expenditure control system designed to help
the faculty researcher monitor research projects. The faculty
member first establishes a budget for a project; expenditures are
coded for application to a budget category. At the end of each
month, I receive a copy of the budget, expenditures to date, and
the uncommitted balance. It is also possible to encumber funds;
for example, salaries for research assistants working on a project
appear for the entire year at one time. Beyond the summary sheet,
there are monthly detailed reports of each charge.

While this system sounds like a useful tool, there are a number
of reasons why the theory behind it has failed in practice. The
primary problem with the system is the long time lag between an
expenditure and its appearance on the report. Sometimes months
go by before something is actually charged against the project, frequently too late to take any action. The second problem is that the
report is extremely difficult to read and understand. As we say, the
user interface—that is, what the user sees when working with
the system—is terrible. There is a half-day course that is given to
explain how to use the report; there must be a problem when it

takes half a day to explain the use of what is usually a one or two page report.

As a result of these difficulties, our local accounting office has started to keep a duplicate system. It posts charges to accounts and modifies the computer-generated control reports to update them manually prior to distribution. An interesting man-machine system!

The Required Inventory Example

No list of examples of computer systems would be complete without the inclusion of an inventory system. Inventory control is one of the computer field's most shining examples of success. Here we can generally demonstrate cost savings through reduced inventory balances and better service levels. Most modern inventory systems not only keep track of stock, they employ some type of mathematical formula to suggest the quantity of a product and the best time to reorder. We have also had considerable success marrying the inventory system to a forecasting routine which predicts total demand for each item in inventory. The demand is an input to formulas which attempt to calculate the best order time and quantity for each item in inventory.

It has even been suggested by the popular press that the combined effect of many computer-based inventory systems has been to reduce the impact of business cycles. To the extent that these systems allow better control over finished goods inventories, the negative impacts of excess stocks during a recession or deficient stocks during an economic expansion have been reduced. That is, firms with better inventory control do not have to sell excess stock at a reduced price during a recession and vice versa. There appears to be no data to support this observation, but it would be nice if it were true.

Of course, there have been inventory systems that fail, just as other systems have encountered problems. One consultant reports a system in which, after careful examination, he found that inventory balances were maximized rather than minimized. There was a small programming error, and management had not carefully examined the results. Keeping track of inventory is a good application of computers; but like everything else, there is a lot of work and careful checking required to develop a system that does what it is supposed to do.

Why Payroll?

True or False: payroll is one of the basic, well-understood tasks in a company. The truth of this statement depends on the person with whom we are speaking. There is a large number of computer department managers who use service bureaus to compute the payroll. Others argue that payroll is a great application because it has high visibility in the firm; a good payroll system is an advertisement to potential users of what the company and the staff can do.

Whatever one's persuasion, payroll is often computer based today. One advantage of computer processing is that the myriad of government reports required can be easily produced from a system which computes the payroll for employees. In the simplest case, payroll takes input transactions of hours worked and multiplies them by the pay rate saved in computer memory. Various deductions and taxes are computed and a check printed.

There are many variations on this theme, of course. For salaried individuals, the payroll requires no inputs except special conditions such as vacation, sickness, and so forth. In the normal case, the computer program produces the same check each period, updating year-to-date totals in memory. For more complex situations, the payroll system may collect hours which are distributed against production records to come up with the cost of goods sold or the labor variance in a standard costing system.

Decision Systems

The academic profession has discovered another type of information system, the decision support system. While there is some debate as to what constitutes one of these applications, most of them seem to be aimed at a relatively well-defined problem area. Typically, the systems are interactive; that is, the user works at a computer terminal which is in direct communication with the system. It is then possible to try a number of different conditions at one sitting. Frequently the computer simulates different options, and the user can pick the results that look the most attractive.

One airline has used such a system to help plan fuel loadings for aircraft. The computer has a model, a representation of the route structure and the price of fuel at various locations. The computer picks the best fueling strategy for the airline. The advantage of the computer system is that it can consider a large number of variables and compute a new solution at will as prices or other conditions change. The airline reported savings of six million dollars a year from the use of the system.

Office Automation

A great deal has been written about the application of computers to the office environment. The basic components of this application include word processing, electronic mail, and text editing. Other options include calendar and reminder systems. A number of computer faculties in universities use these systems, and several firms have installed prototype or completely "automated offices."

Using electronic mail, individuals communicate by means of computer terminals. After someone sends a message, it appears to the recipient at his or her terminal or when he or she logs onto a terminal and establishes communications with the computer. The recipient can read the message then or later and can reply with ease. Multiple copies can be sent to other people's "electronic mailboxes."

Text editing allows the individual to work from a terminal, entering manuscripts and editing them with the help of the computer. Changes such as insertion and deletion of words, rearrangement of sentences and paragraphs, and so on are made easily. After the editing is completed, a word processing system produces high quality printouts from the edited text if desired.

While there is yet no clear indication of its success, most of us in the field feel that the automated office will be a reality within the next five years. Possibly not all features will be implemented, but managers and others will have extensive contact with computers as a part of their daily activities.

A Classification Scheme

We have seen several examples of computers; it would be nice to find some way to classify them for easy reference. Information systems exist to support decision making, controls, and the processing of transactions in the firm. Beginning with decisions, we can describe three categories which are commonly used to characterize information systems. At one extreme we find strategic planning and, at the other, operational control. In the middle are managerial control decisions.

In strategic planning, management sets the objectives and long-range strategy of the firm. Examples of strategic decisions are those to merge with another firm, to open a new subsidiary, or to offer a new product. These decisions are significant and have a long-range impact on the firm. In the earlier example, the market research firm combined technology and strategy to gain a competitive edge in its industry.

With managerial control, we are concerned that the resources of the firm will be used to achieve strategic objectives. Managerial control decisions tend to be involved with financial and personnel matters. A budgeting system is a good example of a managerial control application, as is the university project control system already described.

Operational control decisions are concerned with the day-to-day functioning of the firm. Inventory control systems are perfect illustrations; if the inventory is not kept under control, the firm will be unable to operate. Operational systems require accurate information, and they usually must be quite up-to-date. These applications have typically been some of the first automated in firms.

In addition to providing information for decision making, many computer applications have automated the production of paper, in sectors like banking and insurance, the same way that Henry Ford automated the assembly line in manufacturing. These systems are well understood, highly structured, and often developed early in a firm's experience with computers. Payroll is a good example of this type of system.

What Hath Technology Wrought?

We have now reviewed a few examples of computer applications and should be able to see the tremendous impact this technology has and will have on managers and the firm. There are large central computers and small models that fit on a desk top. The technology has advanced so rapidly that it presents many alternatives, too many for the average user. Earlier I maintained that we have been technology-driven in the field and that key management issues have often been subordinated to the latest technological advance or fad.

My goal in the rest of this book is to help answer questions that the manager has been afraid to ask or unable to have answered. In today's computing environment—marked with steadily decreasing costs for and the concurrent proliferation of computer components—management can and must control information processing in the firm.

CHAPTER 2

How Much Should We Spend on Computing?

MY ACQUAINTANCES WITH two different board chairmen began with the question, "How much should a company our size be spending on computing?" Both men described feelings that they were spending too much for computers and obtaining too little. They felt that computing was out of control. In this chapter we discuss the costs of computing and try to answer the question of how much one should spend. I am sorry that we shall find no definitive guidelines or benchmarks; do not be misled by biased samples and easily quoted numbers. We shall discuss the components of computing costs and some factors that influence how much the firm is likely to spend on processing.

Processing Costs

There are a number of components to the cost of computing for an organization. Before examining these parts in detail, we must distinguish between a general-purpose computer operation and a dedicated application which may occur on a mini- or microcomputer.

Two Polar Extremes

In the early days of computing, the customer bought or rented a general-purpose computer. The firm established a data processing (DP) department and hired a staff of operators, programmers, systems analysts, and clerks. The analysts developed the logic and design of a computer application, such as payroll or accounts payable, and programmers wrote the necessary computer code for the system to run. The operators and clerks actually ran the system on a routine basis, balanced report totals, and distributed the output. Today there are many companies with computer centers providing this type of service.

With the advent of an inexpensive, small, mini- or microcomputer, a number of organizations have purchased computer systems that are dedicated to one application like order entry. Typically, a software vendor develops a set of package programs to do some application. I have recently worked with one such vendor who offers a complete order entry, inventory control, product allocation, shipping invoicing, and accounts receivable system on-line (users work interactively with terminals) for the garment manufacturing industry. The software vendor buys the computer and installs the system at the client's site, making minor modifications in the input and output to suit the unique needs of the client.

With this kind of dedicated system, the user does not require a large computer department. If few modifications or extensions are required, there may even be no need for a programmer. However, the vendor does recommend that there be one person who is responsible for the system on a full-time basis. A specialist helps the user when there are problems and develops new reports and special inquiries.

We see two points on a continuum: the large, general-purpose installation and the small, dedicated system. Both will have similar cost categories, but the distribution of expenditures for each budget category will differ for each type of installation.

Hardware and Software

One major cost component is hardware, the actual computer device we can see, the computing equipment which may be purchased, rented, or leased. The firm may buy packaged software, that is, programs that have been written by a firm to sell for general use to others. For installations that write their own programs, the cost of purchased software will be relatively small. (The customer usually must buy or rent computer languages and special development aids.) However, writing one's own software requires an expensive staff of systems analysts and programmers.

The most important change in the computing field has been in hardware; prices have declined while performance has improved dramatically. In the early days of computing, the hardware might represent 50 percent of the annual DP department budget. For the large, general-purpose installation today the number is probably closer to 25 percent. At the same time, the cost of software has increased dramatically due to increasing salaries and the demand for more computer applications.

The decline in cost of computing and the increase in capacity means that we no longer need to consider the hardware a scarce resource. Too often we still design applications for the benefit of the computers, i.e., to save computer time or to require less computing power. Given the continuing trends of reductions in price with increases in power, we should view hardware as an abundant resource and design systems that are responsive to users.

Communications

The first computer applications ran in batch mode; all input was collected at one point in time; the system updated and printed reports produced for distribution. This cycle might occur monthly, for example, with a budgeting application. Today, there are many on-line systems where we use terminals at different locations to communicate with a computer. Often different computers communicate with each other. There are a variety of ways for such communications to occur, but all of them involve some cost. The cost of a nationwide communications network can be a large component of the total cost of computing.

Staff

For most organizations, the number of computer department staff members is growing in order to meet high demands for service. At the same time, salary costs are increasing rapidly due to inflation in general and the extremely short supply of computer professionals. Staff costs are expected to continue to escalate in the future.

Supplies

Any operation requires various supplies. In the computer area we need relatively expensive paper, tapes, and disks and other miscellaneous items.

Installation

Computers must be located someplace; for the small, dedicated system the space and environmental requirements are quite modest. The larger, general-purpose computer usually needs raised flooring for cables and special air-conditioning. This component of cost may require a substantial initial investment and an ongoing expense for electricity, maintenance, overhead, and so forth.

The Total Cost

Now we have seen the major components of processing costs. What can be said about how this total should compare to some figure like company sales? I can offer some very broad guidelines but they should not be regarded as definitive.

Why One Might Spend More

There are a number of factors which are likely to be associated with higher expenditures for information processing (see Table 2-1). Unfortunately, there is at present no way to measure these variables and compute what a reasonable range of DP expenditures might be for a specific firm. However, if you consider how your situation fits the following factors, you might better gauge in broad terms how important computing is to the firm and where your firm might stand in comparison with others regarding processing expenditures.

Uncertainty in the Environment

From a theoretical point of view, we suggest that one role of information is to reduce uncertainty. If we had a perfect sales forecast, then there would be little uncertainty in what to manufacture. The more uncertain a firm's environment, the more we would expect it to spend on information processing.

Consider a firm in the semiconductor industry. The environ-

TABLE 2-1 Factors Associated with Relatively Large Computer Budgets

High levels of uncertainty in the environment	Membership in an information intense industry
Highly complex business	Large amount of clerical processing
Significant competition	

ment is dynamic and constantly changing as new products are developed and brought to the market. There is a constant need to reduce manufacturing costs and to respond to the changing needs of customers. Here we expect to find high expenditures on information to help reduce uncertainty from the environment.

Complexity

Complex operations themselves generate uncertainty. I have been working with a firm that manufactures one billion pieces a year, admittedly of relatively small value each. Yet there are performance specifications which must be met by the product. Ignoring for a moment environmental uncertainty, the complexity of manufacturing this product (over 30 steps) and the large quantities involved create a lot of internal uncertainty.

In order to cope with such complexity and uncertainty, the firm uses extensive on-line computer systems. These systems keep track of the state of production, process orders, schedule future production, and control shipping. The tremendous complexity of operations generates the need to process information on orders, work in process, manufacturing process, finished goods, and so on.

Competition

In a highly competitive environment, the organization may invest heavily in computing to meet the competition. Banking is an example of an industry with such competition, especially at the retail level. Banks offer new services to customers that probably could never be justified for other than marketing reasons.

When one institution installs a system to dispense cash automatically for a customer, other banks soon follow. The same is true for many other firms in a competitive environment. The manufacturing firm discussed above is planning to install terminals in the offices of general distributors so they can place orders directly. This move is being considered because its major competition has done so already, making it easy for the distributors to order from them.

Nature of the Industry

The very nature of the business may lead to a heavy investment in computing. The most obvious example is firms in the business of supplying data to customers. Credit bureaus and rating agencies are major computer users. Firms in this sector of the economy have adopted computers and made their data available instantly to a customer with a computer terminal who connects to the central computer and its data bank.

Clerical Intensity

Earlier, we observed that computers have been used to process millions of transactions, turning paperwork into an assembly-line type of operation. Banks and insurance firms spent large amounts on computing because of their extensive requirements to process transactions. We would expect a high level of expenditures, then, in industries characterized by a high volume of transactions and intense clerical activity.

The Bottom Line

It would be nice at this point to state a formula in which the reader might insert values and compute the "proper" level of expenditures for information processing. I am unable to do so. But is there a role for benchmarks and to what extent are they credible?

Many years ago a leading business publication presented an article claiming that a survey had shown the average manufacturing firm spent something like 1.4 percent of its sales on computing. The chairman of the board of a French firm was most upset because his company was spending 1.5 percent and I had great difficulty in focusing his attention away from the "extra" 0.1 percent and onto the real problems his firm had with its information systems.

Please do not use statistics in this manner. The amount to invest in computing is a function of many complex factors, and the range of expenditures among companies will be large. A firm in research may have a large budget, a small company may have no computing at all. One large insurance firm spends over 10 percent of its operating budget on computing!

Probably the most useful statistics are averages for your industry, (published by a trade association for example) since many of the items above are influenced by the type of business one is in, e.g., uncertainty, complexity, or clerical intensity. If industry figures show that you are at the bottom in information processing expenditures, you may be (1) highly efficient or (2) missing some rather significant opportunities. If, on the other hand, you are at the top of your industry in computer expenditures, then (1) you may be a leader in new and creative computer use or (2) you may be very inefficient.

Simple measures and numbers will not help determine what to do, but these comparisons may give us a starting place. One must try to evaluate the effectiveness of information processing, a most difficult task. In the rest of this book, we will discuss some guidelines to gauge the effectiveness of information processing and will make suggestions for how to gain more control over this activity. If management is effective in directing information processing, then individual expenditures will be justified and the question of how much to spend in the aggregate should be reduced in importance.

CHAPTER 3

Why Do Other Companies Seem to Use Computers Better than We Do?

AT FIRST I FOUND IT amusing when firms where I requested permission to do research responded, ''You don't want to use us as an example, we've got a lot of problems. I am sure there are other places where things are being done right.'' As I encountered this response from more and more firms, my amusement changed to concern.

Certainly, ''the grass is always greener,'' but why are there so few shining examples of outstanding information-processing activities? Finally, I thought I had found a good example and I referred to it for several years. The manager of this computer department was a senior vice-president of the firm and a member of several top management committees. Users seemed extremely satisfied with information-processing services. The company had on-line, batch, and interactive time-sharing systems. New applications were developed quickly and worked well.

Then one day the roof fell in. I talked with the manager and found that a shift in senior management had precipitated a crisis. Users with new influence and power were now trying to embarrass him. A consulting firm had been summoned to evaluate the computing operation and to make recommendations. Top management told the computer manager to change his approach. And so I lost my example of a successful computing operation, but I suspect the company has lost a great deal more.

Why Then Does It Seem that Others Do It Better?

My conclusion after a number of years is that others are *not* necessarily doing the job better, we only perceive that they are. But why?

The Highly Visible Application

We often hear about or read a description of a very advanced and exciting system. There are two things to watch here: first, the description may be exaggerated. I remember visiting a company where, after talking with users, I felt that computers were being used effectively. The firm was conservative and generally promoted from within. When I interviewed the one manager brought in recently from the outside, he explained that users were happy, but not necessarily for the reason I suspected. He asked, "Did they show you the room where clerks take the computer printout and type or write up a report manually in the same format as before the computer?" Watch the press accounts of systems carefully, there may be less than meets the eye!

Second, we must be wary of the fallacy of the highly visible application because there are usually few of these in number compared to the total number of applications in any one firm. There may be one or even two quite advanced systems, but what kind of service is received by the majority of users?

Criteria

If we think others have good systems, what criteria have we used in evaluating and reporting on them? Often the popular data-processing literature relishes the technology, never mind the effectiveness of the resulting system. As an industry, we lack standards or clear evaluation criteria for systems.

When I evaluate systems, my focus is on what they accomplish for the organization and on the user reaction to the application. What is management's subjective evaluation of the firm's computing effort? How are systems designed and what is the role of management, users, and the professional computer staff in their design?

The Service Business

Computing is a service business, a difficult line of work to be in. Users of services frequently complain about providers, no matter what the nature of the service. I have no favorite airlines, only some that are "acceptable" and a long list of those I try to avoid if at all possible. Fortunately, I do not fly every day. In a typical firm, however, people use computing services daily or even continuously.

Trying to provide these services is not a simple task. The manager of information processing is confronted with the creative activity of systems analysis and design and the mundane requirements of running a job shop to operate systems on a regular basis. It is hard to please in this environment.

Personal Factor

For reasons of economy and because we do not always understand very well how people use information, we have tended to design one-dimensional systems. That is, systems that support a group of people in a single function produce the identical report for each individual. As we saw earlier, there are a variety of factors that influence how people interpret data to turn it into information.

A report may look exciting and relevant to a systems analyst but is not well regarded by the user. The analyst who describes a system at another firm in glowing terms may not realize that users there are highly critical of the system.

Pieces, but Not the Whole

Things may seem better at other organizations because we tend not to see the whole picture. The typical user sees a few applications in his or her functional area of the firm, finance, accounting, or others. Rarely does one user or manager understand or appreciate the full range of computer applications in the organization.

How about the manager of the information service department? This individual may know subconsciously the range of applications and users served, but there are usually only a few applications commanding his attention. The systems of most interest are (1) new applications, especially where there are problems like cost and budget overruns, (2) applications with a high backlog of requests for change, and (3) systems which are experiencing operating problems.

In short, the manager of information processing is often a fire fighter; it is difficult for one in this position to plan or to think about the implications of the firm's large number of computer applications. Even though the company is critically dependent on computers to stay in business, no one may really appreciate that fact.

Conclusions

My conclusion is that chances are the other company is doing no better overall than you are! The other firm may have more glowing press and public relations, but what is important is how effective your systems are for you.

The collective experience of many other firms and a large number of applications may be a useful reference point in evaluating your own processing effort. Some firms have successfully used an outside reviewer who can ask penetrating questions about decisions regarding computers and can help management evaluate the technical advice it receives from within. The outsider can also act as a sounding board for new applications and new directions being considered by the computing department and as an agent to help transfer new technologies to the firm.

The role of the outside reviewer described above is a difficult one. The consultant must establish credibility with senior management and with the systems group. At times the consultant will make a recommendation unpopular to both groups and the advice may go unheeded.

An external view is not mandatory and there undoubtedly are organizations that do not need it. But as one manager of information processing put it, ''We need an insurance policy—a view from the outside to help us and to help management feel comfortable with what we are doing. And we need advice so that we in the computer area feel comfortable with our own decisions.''

CHAPTER 4

How Do I Know if Things Are Going Well?

BECAUSE OF THE NEWNESS of the technology and their lack of familiarity with it, managers have a great deal of difficulty knowing whether or not their information services departments are functioning adequately. There seem to be few indicators for diagnosing problems or even for determining whether problems exist.

Danger Signals

There are ten symptoms in an organization which usually are signs that management needs to take corrective action to gain control over information processing.

1. *User complaints about service levels.* The information processing activity is a service; if users complain chronically about the level of service they receive, then there is good cause for alarm. Naturally, services can always be better; however, I have observed vastly differing levels of user satisfaction among information processing departments. If user complaints are the rule rather than

the exception, management should look further into the reasons for the complaints.

2. *Hostile attitudes toward the computer staff.* Attitudes are a good predictor of how people behave. If users are highly antagonistic toward the computer staff, it will be hard to foster cooperation to resolve problems or to gain cooperation in the design of a system. I have seen companies in which user attitudes were so negative that users would not speak to someone associated with the computer field.

3. *Fatalistic and demoralized computer staff members.* When relations are poor in a firm, the computer staff begins to react to negative user attitudes. As a result, the staff adopts an attitude of "what does it matter what we do—they are dead set against computers." Chronic lack of success perceived by the staff increases turnover and lowers morale. The negative feelings of users will be reciprocated and there will be a steady downward trend in the relationship between users and the computer staff.

4. *Lack of contribution of systems to critical activities of the firm.* Information systems have an important role to play in the organization. If these systems do not support key areas of the business, something is wrong. For example, I have heard of firms where the information services department developed new computer applications for a product that was about to be taken off the market! If systems support mundane and unimportant activities, management needs to redirect the information-processing effort.

5. *No idea of where system development is headed.* If management does not have a picture of the kind of future systems desired, then it will be at the mercy of competing demands for new applications in the firm. Without a clear plan, it is likely that a variety of applications will be suggested and approved, though the applications may not support key areas of the business.

6. *Discomfort with the procedures for identifying new applications.* Managers frequently complain that systems proposals are always approved. There seems to be no rationale for selecting a particular application that has been recommended by users and the computer staff. Management does not play an active role in identifying critical applications of the computer. Managers may

approve the budgets, but have the feeling that they are acting as a "rubber stamp" for decisions that have actually already been made at a lower level of the organization.

7. *One or more applications experiencing significant cost and/or budgeting overruns.* The field has not had conspicuous success in achieving estimates on cost or time for the development of new applications. However, if overruns are the rule, then something is wrong with the estimation process or with the management of projects. A system must be managed, the staff must be able to make the technology work, and users must be involved to develop and implement a new computer application. If there are cost and time overruns, management should probe deeply to find out the reasons for these results.

8. *Continual requests for more computer staff and computer equipment.* It seems that the information processing budget rises regardless of whether any new applications are implemented. Some of the increase in budget is due to increasing demand for new applications and improvements in existing systems. However, is there some return for this investment? Do new staff members reduce the backlog of requests for changes and new systems? Does new equipment improve service levels? One cannot just view their requests or the history of increased expenditures; we also must determine whether the investment has produced the promised results in order to justify additions to the staff and to the equipment base.

9. *Lack of management input on key decisions about information processing.* At what levels are the key decisions about information processing really made? Does management have an input in the areas described above, for example, in the identification of critical applications areas for the firms? Is management actively involved in planning for information processing, or does the computer staff view management as an obstacle to be overcome at budget approval time? To lead, managers must have an input into key decisions like the identification of applications, the structure of computing, the major logic of a new system, the acquisition of new staff and computer equipment, and the evaluation of information processing.

10. *The feeling that information processing, rather than management, controls the organization.* While one can look for examples and evidence, the most important indicator of a problem is how you feel. If you do not feel that management controls information processing, then that feeling alone is a sufficient reason to take action. When managers have the confidence that they control information processing, this technology will make its maximum contribution to the firm.

CHAPTER 5

How Can Top Management Cope with Computing?

IF AN ORGANIZATION IS SUFFERING from several of the symptoms of problems with computing described in the last chapter, it may be depriving itself of the opportunity to invest in information systems as a part of its corporate strategy. Most of the systems we have discussed so far are oriented toward improving the efficiency of the organization. As such, they help the firm accomplish its goals, but in a rather indirect way. We call these Level 1 systems. (See Table 5–1.)

Level 2 systems are those which aid the strategic planning process itself. There are many examples of special computer languages and systems available to help the manager construct a model of the firm. Then one can ask "what if" questions and test different assumptions. This kind of system assists the planner and top management in formulating a strategic plan.

In a level 3 system, the information system actually becomes a part of corporate strategy. Consider the small market research firm described in Chapter 1 that noted the slow implementation rate of point-of-sale scanners in grocery stores. Installing the equipment free in stores in two typical towns allowed the firm to offer precise market research studies to its clients. The market research firm now has an edge over its larger competition due to the innovative use of technology.

TABLE 5-1   Strategy and Information Systems

Level 1	Efficiency, transactions, operational control, managerial control systems
Level 2	Strategic planning systems
Level 3	Information systems as a part of corporate strategy

In another example, a major brokerage firm recognized that it could use computer technology to offer a new service to customers. Prior to the development of a new system, the cash in an individual's brokerage account remained invested at no interest. However, the brokerage firm had a high yield liquid assets fund and it used computer technology to couple the fund to the brokerage account. When an investor has cash in his or her brokerage account, it is now automatically invested in the liquid assets fund at a rate that is considerably higher than even the bank rate.

As a result, the brokerage firm is offering a service which makes trading with it more attractive than with competitors. It also means that the firm's own liquid assets fund is assured a new source of capital; that fund is now one of the largest in existence. By taking advantage of the technology, the company has gained a major competitive advantage.

Such opportunities await many other firms. What has prevented them from taking advantage of them? There are two answers to this question. First, it is very difficult to recognize such strategic opportunities. There is no formula or cookbook that suggests how to employ the technology to gain such an advantage. The other reason why firms do not take full advantage of the technology is more serious: management does not feel confident that it controls information processing in the organization. How can the firm trust its future to a technology that it cannot control?

A Framework

Jon Turner of New York University and I have developed a framework that summarizes the key management policy issues for

FIGURE 5-1   Management Control of Information Processing

controlling information processing in the organization (see Figure 5-1). The purpose of this scheme is to point out the critical areas for management attention and action. We shall present an overview of the framework in this chapter and discuss its components in more detail in subsequent chapters. Through careful attention to the issues raised here, management can gain control of information-processing technology. Given the ability to control the technology, it should be possible to apply information processing to all areas of the business with confidence. No longer will we be afraid to use information systems as a part of corporate strategy because we lack the confidence to manage and control systems.

Planning

The key to gaining control of information processing is to have a plan for systems. This plan should cover a three- to five-year planning horizon and detail the goals and objectives of information processing in the organization. The details of the plan will be the subject of the next chapter.

It is not easy to develop a system plan; often the firm itself lacks a plan. Yet, it is the plan of the firm that determines the kind of computer applications that are needed. Applications in turn are a key component of the plan; they determine the requirements for staff and equipment beyond what exists today.

The need to develop a systems plan may force the firm to document its own plans for the next three years. At a minimum, management must at least verbalize the areas of the business which are to be stressed in the future and participate in the process of identifying new computer applications.

Organization Structure

As we shall see in Chapter 7, the technology has presented a large number of options for providing computing services. We can have centralized computers with access from the entire country or even around the world. We can also have a large number of minicomputers, small computers dedicated to individual users or applications. The large number of choices makes it difficult to develop a structure for the location of equipment and services. Later we will suggest some criteria to be used and present guidelines for making such decisions.

Applications

Users seem to have an insatiable appetite for new computer applications. How does management identify the most promising areas? How do we ration scarce personnel and assign them to important new applications? The field has had problems estimating in advance how long it will take to develop a new computer system and what it will cost. Thus, plans tend to be too optimistic about what can be accomplished. Also, many information services departments fail to add up all of their commitments—and promise more applications than it is possible to develop. We must identify new applications and then determine what will be required to develop them.

Operations

Unfortunately, few computer applications ever go away; it seems that we must operate every system that was ever developed in the firm. Old systems also have a habit of growing as users suggest modifications and enhancements to make them more useful. As a result, we have a steadily increasing demand for computing power to run existing applications.

The operation of existing systems is the primary point of contact between users and the computer department. Providing service is always a difficult assignment and the computer area has proved no exception. There are many complaints with the quality of computing service, and often the problem is with operations. I shall try in a later chapter to present some ideas for monitoring service levels and providing a more effective interface between the computer and users.

Resource Requirements

The demands of new applications and the continuing needs of existing operations combine to determine the needs for equipment and staff. Of the two, it is far easier to add computing power; hardware is becoming less expensive while personnel costs are increasing steadily. Unfortunately, it is not just a matter of cost, but of supply; it may not be possible to recruit the needed computer personnel to accomplish all that is desired. The plan must consider carefully whether or not there are sufficient people available to develop the needed applications.

The desired structure of the organization will help determine the type of computing hardware to be acquired. For example, if the decision is to distribute and decentralize computers, then the organization will probably want to acquire multiple small machines rather than large, central computers.

Charging

One of the most controversial areas in the management of computing is the charging of users for services. First, should we charge at all for computing services, and if so, how much and on what basis? Chapter 16 explores some of the pros and cons of charging and suggests some criteria for a charging scheme if one is adopted.

Control

The final objective of the framework is to gain control over computing. In Chapter 17 I discuss some different measures that can be used to determine whether or not computing is under control. If information processing is not under control, then what actions are available to management to influence it? There are many things that the nontechnical manager can do to influence computing; we shall discuss them further in the rest of the book.

Summary

Computing and information-processing technology offer abundant opportunities to contribute to the strategy of the firm. Our application of this technology as a part of corporate strategy has been limited by our imagination and by the fear that we cannot manage the technology. In this chapter we have presented an overview of critical areas in which management may act to gain control of information processing; in the next few chapters we explore each policy area in more detail. Just as managers are able to control other areas of the business, they can manage information processing.

CHAPTER 6

What's in a Plan for Information Systems?

THERE ARE MANY REASONS why a firm needs a plan for information systems. The plan is the first step in gaining control over information processing; it allows us to forecast the staff and equipment needs of the information-processing area and should help guide orderly growth. One problem top managers face is the escalating need for computer staff and equipment. With a plan, it should be possible to forecast that growth and to make a conscious decision whether the new applications necessitating increased expenditure levels are worthwhile.

The plan also helps users understand where their favorite applications fit in the scheme of things. Obviously, we cannot anticipate every good application, and the plan will have to contain a reserve for contingencies. However, the information services department is generally placed in the position of having to approve or reject requests for new systems; the plan would make it clear where new applications fit. Also, major new applications or changes in key areas can be evaluated partially on the basis of their impact on what has already been planned.

A plan also makes potential accomplishments more evident and, as each new application is sketched and estimates are made, the requirements for resources unfold. In most organizations I have visited, more has been promised in the way of systems than can possibly be delivered. No one has taken the time to total all requirements, to observe that the information-processing area is committed to more than it can accomplish. As an example, one German bank estimated that there were 300 applications in its backlog. A survey found that the number was 600 and that it would take ten years to complete them at the current rate of development.

Finally, the plan is a vital element in monitoring the progress of the information services department. Without a plan, there is no benchmark for management. What is progress? How well is the department performing? With a plan to examine, management can assess one aspect of the performance of the department.

The Planning Process

Planning is not easy, and the nonprogrammed, routine activities of the firm often override plans. We recognize that a plan is desirable, but everyday crises and fire-fighting always seem to get in the way. Sometimes the manager of the information services department is told to develop a plan; but if the organization lacks a plan, this task will be very difficult. We would like to have a reasonably explicit plan for the firm as a starting point. Then the manager of the information services department, along with users and management, can develop a plan for information systems.

Either through a strategic plan for the firm or by some other means, top management should communicate the areas of the business that are expected to grow and to receive emphasis during the next five years. Top management helps set the key applications areas for future development. It is not wise to invest resources in some part of the business which is going to contract or even be eliminated. Usually top management alone has the knowledge necessary to make decisions on key applications areas.

For an information services plan to work, it must be well publicized; important individuals in the firm have to influence its development. The plan cannot be a document drawn up exclusively by the manager of the computer department. I generally recommend a task force consisting of key managers working with the manager of the information services department to prepare a plan. These managers can involve subordinates at their discretion. The plan needs to be a consensus document to the greatest extent possible, since we are trying to allocate scarce resources among individuals with competing demands. It is a very poor practice to ask the manager of the information services department to make such a resource trade-off; this individual needs the cooperation of those who are asking for services. Forcing the decision on the information services manager makes it difficult to establish rapport with users whose requests have been refused or delayed.

Over time, probably each year, the plan needs to be updated and modified. There may be innovations in the technology that cause previously marginal applications to become desirable. New priorities may have arisen, or projects under way may have encountered problems requiring more resources or rescheduling. The same mechanism involving key managers should be employed to make changes and updates to the plan.

An Example

Despite the number of articles about planning, there is no formula for a plan. Each organization has unique requirements. In the rest of this chapter, I present the outline of a plan that was developed by a large insurance firm; parts of it should be applicable in other organizations. This particular company had lagged seriously in the development of systems. It had saved money on computing, but was being constrained because present systems would not let it develop new lines of business and grow in new directions.

Planning in this firm was made difficult by the lack of an overall plan for the company. There was a management group which had been convened to oversee the information-processing area; I suggested that the group develop a plan to determine what kinds of improvements in processing were feasible. The chairman of the firm was a very strong figure who frequently changed his mind about both policy and operational issues. One of my motives in suggesting the development of a plan came from the impression that resources were totally inadequate to accomplish even part of what was being suggested by the manager of the information-processing area and the supervisory committee.

Executive Summary

The plan began with a short executive summary. As we expected the entire document to be quite lengthy, an overall summary was necessary to communicate with top management and to encourage individuals to examine the details.

Goals

The firm basically operated batch-transactions processing systems. There were few real master files, much less a data base. The files consisted of magnetic tapes of transactions; management reports required programs to summarize all of the transactions on tape. The computer area was considered a disaster by most users and top management.

The goals of the plan were essential, then, to gaining acceptance and commitment from users. Just as one might expect in a situation like this, users were quick to blame the computer department for any problems and unwilling to undertake the tasks necessary for successful systems.

The insurance firm operated around the world. After careful consideration, the supervisory committee decided that a goal would be to move systems closer to the end user; this strategy meant the establishment of regional computer centers and a movement toward more on-line systems for input. Because there were significant problems with data entry from unskilled clerical personnel in different countries, on-line input was also felt to be important for its immediate editing and error-feedback capabilities.

Assumptions

The chairman of this firm did not like to write down plans; his one clear goal was a 20 percent increase each year in sales and profits. The plan made this assumption a basis for projecting increases in business and information-processing requirements.

Scenario

In this section we sketched a scenario of what different users would encounter in the way of computer support. The purpose of the scenario was to make abstract policy statements concrete, to bring the goals closer to reality by describing the environment that would result from implementing the plan.

The scenario was nontechnical and could easily be understood by a user and/or manager who would be asked to help develop and use systems described in the scenario. In retrospect, the scenario was an extremely important part of the plan because it was possible for the reader to relate to it and to understand what the implications of the plan were for him or her.

Applications

This section of the plan outlined the major applications that were under way or which were desired by users in the firm. This was a key section of the plan and a very large one. The information-processing staff developed a common format for descriptions of current or intended projects and their resource requirements. Though this task was never completed for reasons discussed later, I was fairly certain that it would show an impossibly high level of staff required to implement the plan.

The supervisory committee was also important in this task. It was necessary to delineate the major applications that had been requested or that were needed in the immediate future. Users and managers have the knowledge to make such a determination, not the computer department staff. The identification of key areas for new applications, then, is a task that must be accomplished outside of the information services area.

Operations

Because of the large number of new applications, the plan had significant implications for computer operations. As one might suspect, with such a poor history of information processing, current operations were precarious. The present manager of the computer area had spent most of his first year putting operations into order. Based on his description of the situation in operations when he took over, the firm was close to being out of business because the computer was being operated with inadequate controls and nonexistent documentation.

For this company, the plan for operations had to include resources to bring existing operations to a minimally acceptable level. Then resources had to be provided to enable the firm to develop and operate the new applications that had been envisioned in the previous section of the plan.

Maintenance and Enhancements

Research results indicate that organizations spend, at a minimum, about half of their systems development budget on maintenance and enhancements. Fortunately, most of these enhancements make a system more useful. We do not know to what extent it is possible to foresee user demands that generate requests for enhancements during design and how much is learned through the actual use of a system. The consequences are that we often have relatively little staff resources to use in the development of new systems since so much manpower is devoted to modifying existing systems.

On the other hand I have suggested, not entirely facetiously, that if we have a system with no maintenance or enhancements for six months, we should consider discontinuing it because probably no one is using it. We must expect to change systems as people use them and as business or environmental conditions change. Thus, a plan will have a budget for maintenance and enhancements.

Organizational Structure

There are a variety of ways to organize information-processing services. The availability of a variety of computing devices and communications presents many alternatives. Similarly, we can organize the computing staff in a number of different patterns. For the insurance company, the plan to distribute more processing to users included the development of regional computer centers. Since much of the data for a region or even country is local, it appeared that a cost analysis would result in favor of local operations connected to a central site for transmission of financial summary data and other information.

The plan should discuss the pattern of processing that will result from the acquisition of equipment and the structure of the organization to support it. This is the place to mention the formation of special task forces, steering committees, and user-liaison representatives. In Chapters 7 and 8 we shall discuss some of the options for organization and suggest criteria that can be used to evaluate them.

Impact of the Plan

The purpose of information systems is to change and improve the way we process information. Such a simple statement has immense implications for the organization. What will be the impact of these changes? Will we need to reorganize some functions, create new departments, or change the way we think about doing a particular job?

A plan is also likely to have a financial impact on the firm. First there is the actual cost of the plan, followed by any accompanying costs of reorganization. Individual systems may also have an impact on costs. Frequently transactions-processing systems save clerical labor or eliminate the need for additional employees as the workload expands. Systems may also change the nature of the way we do business; for example, they may generate additional revenue. The plan should describe the anticipated impact of the activities it includes.

Implementation Risks

An ambitious plan for information processing will have risks. Key projects may not prove feasible, it may be difficult to keep all projects on schedule, or we may not be able to find enough skilled personnel to execute the plan. Users and management may not be ready to participate to the extent required for development of new systems. It is also possible that the changes envisioned in the plan are of such magnitude that the organization cannot cope with all of them. These implementation obstacles may well require parts of the plan to be postponed, projects to be stretched out, or a reduction in the scope of the entire plan.

The End

The sketch of a plan in this chapter was intended to give a feeling for the organization of a plan in one firm. Other plans might need a subset of these headings or entirely different subject headings. However, it is hoped that the example has shown that the objective of a plan is to communicate, to state the base line from which we are beginning, and to show where we would like to be in the future. To implement the plan will require resources which must be detailed. The plan should include key applications areas and should pay attention to the ongoing requirements for operations, maintenance, and enhancements. Finally, we should assess the impact of the plan on the organization and the obstacles that may impede its implementation.

How did the firm in the example use its plan? I am sorry to say that the chairman was impatient; rather than wait for the completion of the plan, he hired a new director of information processing. At that point a new management structure was imposed, and I do not know today if the firm has a plan or if there has been any improvement in information processing. The information I have heard indicates that there has been little or no progress.

We failed to sell the concept of planning to the top manager of the firm, a manager who was not in favor of written plans to begin with. In other organizations I have tried to be sure that a plan is supported by top management; I have found its development a useful exercise. A plan can help a great deal in establishing management control over information processing.

CHAPTER 7

How Should We Organize Computing in Our Firm?

IN THE EARLY DAYS of computing, there were few choices. A firm installed a computer and ran its applications on it. When there was no longer enough capacity, a new computer with more power was acquired. When the third generation of computers appeared in 1964, there appeared to be economies of scale from centralizing the different computer sites that had grown up so far, for example, in different plants.

During the third generation we saw the development of minicomputers which again changed the available options for processing. These inexpensive machines made it possible to acquire a computer and dedicate it to one task or to a small group of users. The desire to connect a number of computers into a network that could share the processing load and communicate data led to distributed processing.

As a result of these trends, we have a large number of alternatives for configuring computers in an organization. While the options present us with a great deal of flexibility, they complicate the task of choosing a structure. In this chapter we shall discuss some of the different possibilities and offer criteria for evaluating a pattern.

The Continuum

The computing function involves far more than just equipment; too often we have let the technology dictate what should be management decisions. In addition to equipment, we are interested in the location of information and the location of the information services department, particularly the systems analysis and design function. The three variables then are:

1. Information

2. Equipment

3. Computer staff

Each of these components can be centralized or decentralized.

Since *distributed* is a popular word, we shall digress a moment to define it. Often today there is confusion between distributed and decentralized processing. In a sense, decentralization is more radical than distribution; total decentralization means that the local user has complete control over information processing equipment, information, and the systems staff.

Distributed processing usually means that various computers are connected through a communications network. With distributed processing there is some kind of central control and coordination so that information can be exchanged on the network and so that the computers can communicate with each other.

Prototypical Configurations

Table 7-1 shows the values of the three preceding variables on a continuum of centralized to decentralized. Combining the alternatives for each of the three variables yields eight "pure" configurations of processing structures. Of the eight alternatives in the table, only six are generally found; we can eliminate C and G.

The first prototype remaining is one of the most common: centralized equipment, staff, and information. A good example of this type of system is a batch processing operation at a central

TABLE 7-1   Organizational Design for Information Services

	1 / A	2 / B	C	3 / D	4 / E	5 / F	G	6 / H
Information Equipment	Centralized	Decentralized	Centralized	Decentralized	Centralized	Decentralized	Centralized	Decentralized
	Centralized	Centralized	Centralized	Centralized	Decentralized	Decentralized	Decentralized	Decentralized
Computer Staff	Centralized	Centralized	Decentralized	Decentralized	Centralized	Centralized	Decentralized	Decentralized
Example	Very Common, e.g., Batch Systems	Common, e.g., On-Line Systems	Rare	Unusual, e.g., On-Line Systems Local Computer Dept.	Common, e.g., Data Collection from Remote Sites	Computer Staff, Management Coordinates Decentralized Operations	Rare	No Coordination, Complete Local Autonomy
High Coordination Costs				x	x	x		x
Responsiveness		x		x		x		
Special Integration Needed	x	x						x

SOURCE: From "Alternative Structures for the Management of Information Processing," by Henry C. Lucas, Jr., in *The Economics of Information Processing*, vol. 2, edited by Robert Goldberg and Harold Lorin. Copyright © 1982 by John Wiley & Sons, Inc. Used [as edited] by permission.

computer site. The second configuration features centralized staff and equipment but decentralized information. Such a facility is created by the addition of on-line systems and remote inquiry to central computer equipment. The third pattern is central computing but decentralized staff and information. It is unusual, but we might find on-line systems and local computer departments for certain tasks.

The fourth structure features decentralized equipment with centralized staff and information. This type of system is fairly common and is represented by a data collection function with decentralized computers. The information collected is sent to a centralized management group which makes the major decisions.

The fifth prototype includes decentralized equipment and information with centralized management. This structure is typical of an organization with many divisions and a corporate staff. Management coordinates the decentralized operations of the information services function.

The last structure features total decentralization. Here there is no coordination and complete local autonomy is the rule. Information is available only at the local level.

Evaluation Criteria

How does one choose from among the various alternative structures? There are many different reasons why an organization should choose one configuration or another; there can be no single rule for what is best for all firms. The bottom half of Table 7-1 suggests three general evaluation criteria; other factors will have to be developed and evaluated by each organization.

Coordination costs are the costs of assuring that systems and staff members work together. The greater the degree of decentralization, the higher the costs of coordination—until the case where everything is totally decentralized and we do not try to coordinate.

As an example, consider the case of a partially decentralized operation with some communications, a manufacturing firm with several plants. Each of the plants has its own computer communicating with a central computer at corporate headquarters. These separate computers must be coordinated with the central machine. If they are all sending financial information to headquarters, then it will be more efficient if they supply the data in the same format.

From a cost standpoint, we want to avoid having each plant develop the same application; it would be wasteful for the first plant to develop its own payroll system and the second plant to create the same type of system in a parallel effort. Thus, we want to coordinate systems development by looking for opportunities to develop common systems. In conclusion, the greater the degree of decentralization, in general, the greater the coordination costs.

What systems are most responsive to the user? In theory, it seems that if we are able to provide good processing service, it would not really matter where computers are located. From the limited research to date, however, it appears that users feel they receive better service if they have control over equipment.

I explored this feeling with a plant manager who had recently moved from a company with local minicomputers to a firm with a more centralized system. He wanted to have his own computer department and minicomputer. He related that, in his old job, there was a mini and four systems staff members reporting to him. I asked whether or not it was the presence of the equipment or the fact that there were four analysts under his control that made this option seem better. After thinking about it, the manager responded that it was having four people responding to his priorities.

Thus, I fear that there is a tendency to equate the presence of equipment with the ability to control information processing and make it responsive. Control will not necessarily occur just because equipment is present; in fact, the real myth of distributed processing is user control. A major distributed system may actually give users less control because a central site wants to set standards for the distributed equipment and systems. Most local systems will be specified by a central group, in order to maintain compatibility among various hardware and software components.

For the configurations which are primarily centralized, it can be more difficult to provide responsive service. In these instances, there may be a need for special integration. The need for liaison representatives between the computer staff and users is a likely cost for this degree of centralization.

What Should We Do?

All of the above discussion is fine, but how does one go about selecting a processing structure? The first task is to set the strategy of the information services area. What are the goals to be accomplished? What is the history of service? How do users feel about processing? Decide in what direction the information-processing area needs to move and then develop a plan to implement the strategy.

It is important to establish management and user commitment to the goals of a plan, for example, providing more end-user service, moving to on-line processing, creating a data-base environment, or similar items. The decision regarding where to physically place computer equipment can be based on technological and cost considerations combined with consideration of the present location of computers.

If the current computing structure is characterized by a large number of disparate sites which may have grown either without thought to compatibility or through the acquisition of different divisions, then we may want to centralize management in order to coordinate and avoid duplication. The centralized staff will want to consider whether we can change the equipment policy without appearing to offer less responsive service to users.

On the other hand, if we are currently highly centralized and are experiencing major complaints about responsiveness and service levels, then providing some kind of local influence over computing is a good move. This local influence may consist of systems analysts reporting to local management or even some kind of computing equipment under the control of the manager.

Summary

There is no one best way to organize the staff or one best configuration of computers. I have tried to outline some of the options and the design variables which management can influence. The biggest problem in computing today is probably the feeling that systems and the department are unresponsive to users. Users do report more satisfaction with local equipment, but if we could provide good computing service it would not really matter where computers were located. There are other ways to improve service besides giving the user a computer which he must then manage. In general, to improve service I favor working with the management structure, the location of staff, and the types of policies for user involvement in key decisions instead of the location of equipment.

We should decide where to locate computers based on technological and cost factors and concentrate on providing responsive service no matter what the configuration of the equipment. Otherwise, we shall distribute or decentralize processing and forget that responsive service means far more than having one's own computer.

CHAPTER 8

How Can We Organize Our Computer Department?

ONCE A GENERAL STRUCTURE for information processing has been determined, the next question is how to organize within an information services department. In this chapter we shall present the structure for a typical centralized department at one location. It should be possible to make changes in this structure to accommodate different situations, for example, the presence of systems analysts in user departments.

There are a number of tasks undertaken by the typical computer department. The most frequent breakdown is between systems analysis and design and operations. However, we shall see that there are other specialties which must be taken into account when developing the computer organization. Figure 8–1 is an organization chart for a prototypical computer department.

Operations

The operations side of the computer department is responsible for operating existing computer systems. Users see the results of operations on a daily basis. Operations are characterized by heavy

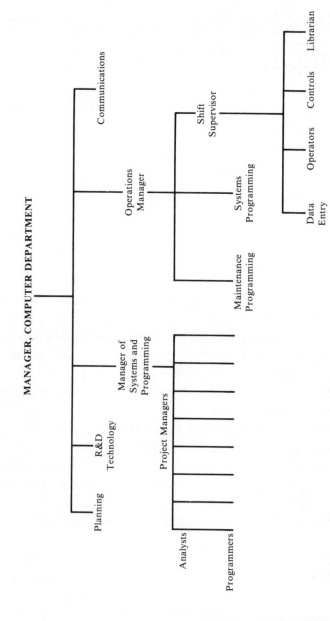

MANAGER, COMPUTER DEPARTMENT

Planning

R&D
Technology

Manager of
Systems and
Programming

Project Managers

Analysts

Programmers

Maintenance
Programming

Operations
Manager

Systems
Programming

Shift
Supervisor

Data
Entry

Operators

Controls

Librarian

Communications

FIGURE 8-1 Typical Computer Department Organization

pressures and deadlines; an hour's delay can make the difference between a good or a bad job.

For batch processing, the operations area represents a classic manufacturing job shop. There are a certain number of jobs and computers capable of running them. The jobs must be scheduled and managed through completion. For on-line applications, the computer system must be kept in operation. Key files of data must be backed up, that is, copies have to be made periodically and stored in a safe place. When the machine fails for a hardware or software reason, the staff must get it back on-line as quickly as possible with minimal disruption.

The typical operations structure for accomplishing these tasks is shown in Figure 8-1. There is a manager of operations with several shift supervisors reporting to him or her. There is a data entry section that keys data into the computer. Computer operators actually run computers; they monitor on-line systems and execute batch jobs according to a schedule set up by the supervisor or a scheduler. There is usually a controls section to check that various run totals balance and that output reports are correct before they are distributed to users. The librarian maintains the library of tapes and disks, devices which store data. (This may sound trivial, but consider the Social Security computer center which has some 500,000 reels of tape!)

Systems Analysis and Design

Systems analysis and design differ greatly from operations. Individuals who work in this capacity tend to think deeply about problems; there is less action than in operations. Much time is spent in meetings and unstructured discussion as different processing alternatives are discussed. Projects typically take a long time to complete; usually there are project teams. The systems design staff considers itself to be professionals, and generally its members have a much higher level of education than do operations personnel.

The typical organization for this group in Figure 8-1 forms a matrix. There is a manager of systems and programming and various project managers. Systems analysts and programmers work on different projects. They report to the manager of systems and programming and to the managers for the various projects on which they are working.

Other Components

In addition to systems analysis and design, there are several other specialties represented in the typical computer department.

Maintenance programming may be located under systems analysis or operations. These individuals are responsible for correcting problems in systems that are already running; they also make enhancements to existing systems when requested by users. Maintenance and enhancements take, on the average, about 50 percent of the total budget for systems analysis and programming.

Systems programmers are responsible for maintaining the control programs that manage the computer. These programs are typically provided by the computer manufacturer and are known as supervisory or operating systems. The systems programming specialty is a narrow and highly paid one.

The manager of the computer department may also have a planner or planning staff reporting to him or her. There may be, in larger departments, a technology or R&D group which is responsible for determining trends in computing devices or planning for equipment to support new applications.

Finally, as we see more on-line systems in which users communicate with the computer from various locations and more computer networks, it is necessary to have communications specialists on the staff. These individuals are responsible for finding the best mix of communications services for the firm from a large number of alternatives. There are constantly changing tariffs and new entrants in the field of communications services so that a full-time staff soon becomes necessary.

Finally, we have the manager of the entire computer department. I believe that this is one of the most difficult jobs in a modern organization; this individual must manage groups with widely differing job tasks and orientations. The environment ranges from one of research, systems design, and planning to the immediate and unceasing pressures of daily operations. At the same time, the manager of the department must relate well to other managers and must help form a liaison with various users. Finally, the manager of information services must be able to work well with the senior management of the organization.

Where Should They Report?

Several weeks ago the chairman of a corporation asked me where the manager of the information services department should report. This reporting relationship is a constant problem for many organizations. In the early history of computing, a data-processing department usually began in accounting because the first applications developed were in accounting. Other functional areas complained that they could not get service; accounting always had the first priority.

Because of these problems, I recommend putting information systems in a neutral position in the organization whenever possible. Many firms now have vice-presidents of systems reporting to a president; others have a separate area known as administrative services which can include information processing.

How about the level of reporting? Does it make any sense for information processing to report as high as the president? The answer to this question depends on whether or not the firm makes a significant expenditure on information systems and whether systems are critical to its success. It is not reasonable to expect a function that has two or three applications and costs .05 percent of sales to report to a senior corporate officer.

However, many firms do find that information processing is becoming a very important activity. By having a senior manager with full-time responsibility for this activity, information processing stays up-to-date on corporate goals and objectives. Some of the best-managed information-processing areas with which I have been involved are headed by managers regarded as senior in the firm who are involved in top management decision making.

The biggest deterrent to this high level for the information-processing manager is the personality of the individual himself. A friend in Europe related the following story. His brother-in-law is the president of a large firm; he asked my friend for advice about his firm's computer area. My friend, who had been in the field working for a computer vendor for 20 years, advised him to take a more active role in information systems. "You must talk to the manager of your computer department for at least 20 minutes a week." The president replied that he would rather leave things in chaos than spend that much time with this manager. "I can't really stand him," he said.

The first action here, then, should be to replace the information services manager with someone more tolerable. The reporting relationship I recommended above requires that we find a real manager for information processing, a person who is capable of managing the department and relating well to other senior managers in the firm. I have met and worked with such individuals and there is hope. A manager with some potential is rare enough to be worth your grooming and encouraging to develop into a senior manager. If there is no hope, then it is time to recruit someone who *can* manage the information-processing area and at the same time work effectively as a senior manager of the firm.

CHAPTER 9

Can We Trust the Vendor?

COMPUTER HARDWARE AND SOFTWARE are supplied by outside vendors who wish to sell more equipment and services. At the same time, the vendor realizes that to oversell a customer can be bad practice: excess capacity can be embarrassing and lead to real problems for the customer. The customer, on the other hand, wants to maintain good relations with suppliers so that service levels are high. The vendor is assumed to have a certain degree of expertise and experience in the field. When there are problems with systems, it is quite possible that the vendor can help resolve them. Constantly lurking in the back of the customer's mind, however, is the fact that the vendor needs to sell. To what extent can we trust the vendor to suppress the selling instinct and to offer honest advice?

Customer Preparation

The vendor's assistance is no substitute for doing one's homework. In contemplating the purchase of equipment or programs, customers should first have an idea of what they want to buy.

I have been working with a client whose problems illustrate this point well. The firm was about a decade behind advances in computer systems and top management was growing increasingly disillusioned with computers. Reports were late and inaccurate, and there were constant machine and staff problems.

The company used an old general-purpose computer from one of the major manufacturers. Its own vendor and vendors of other computers, recognizing the opportunity for a sale, had been putting a lot of pressure on the company to acquire a new computer.

My first task, after some initial interviews in the firm, was to send the computer salesmen away for six months. Then we had a two-day seminar on information systems for the key users and the manager of the information-processing department. The seminar was followed up with the development of a systems plan. We held individual interview sessions and group meetings to develop the outline of a series of systems from order entry through financial accounting.

The plans for the systems were put together into a set of specifications which were sent to the vendors and also to some software houses that had packages designed for this industry. We met with the different vendors and saw demonstrations of hardware and, more importantly, the software available on the different computers. As the customer had a limited capability to develop systems himself, software was more important to the customer than the hardware.

After a rather long comparison period of checking references, attending demonstrations at customer sites, and bringing key users in for demonstrations, we finally made a selection. The choice turned out not to be a major computer vendor but a small software house with a relatively simple, but well-designed set of applications that seemed to fit the customer's environment.

The plan and high level specifications we developed for this situation were extremely important. When a vendor made a presentation we had something against which to judge it. We had our own benchmark. Lacking such a plan, the customer can easily be swayed by nice, but unneeded, features offered by the vendor; the plan forced the vendor to respond to our requirements. By involving the ultimate users of the system in its definition and reviews with the vendors, we began to build acceptance of the new system. At this point, we are beginning implementation and I am optimistic about the readiness of the firm for the new computer system.

Keeping the Vendor Honest

In this example, we were undertaking a major acquisition of hardware and software. The important aspects of this were to know what we wanted and then to insist on seeing demonstrations of a system. In fact, one vendor with a very appealing system was eventually ruled out because, though larger and more stable than the vendor selected, it could not demonstrate a complete system. The applications programs were new and likely to contain a lot of errors.

The next important concept is checking to see that other users are satisfied with the system. I do not recommend being a pioneer, unless one is quite experienced and sophisticated in the use of computers. The firm we selected was a turnkey vendor, a small software house that purchases hardware from a major computer vendor, adds applications packages that it develops, and installs the packaged solution for the customer. We were concerned about hardware maintenance under this arrangement, so we contacted two sets of customers. First we visited clients of the turnkey vendor. Then we obtained from the hardware vendor a list of clients using this model computer (regardless of the software running on it) in the geographic area where our machine would be located. These references were checked to be sure that the equipment would be serviced satisfactorily.

Contract Guarantees

When dealing with anyone other than large hardware vendors who have their own fixed contracts, one can often negotiate some contract guarantees. In the situation described above, we negotiated computer performance guarantees, agreements for backup with the vendor, dates for installation, warranties of fitness for the software, access to the programs for possible modification, and a fixed price for a set of changes to customize the system to our requirements.

Such guarantees are hard to obtain from more established vendors, but we did receive some significant concessions from a major hardware vendor in terms of free service and changes to customize the system had we selected them. Do not be afraid to bargain and to make suggestions when involved in a competitive bidding situation.

Ongoing Relations

Once the system is installed, the honeymoon is over. We now enter a continuing relationship with the vendor, and it is important for both parties that it go well. At this point, we have to rely on the vendor for advice, maintenance, and other forms of assistance. In the back of the vendor's mind are possible future sales of hardware or software, hence the importance of servicing the customer.

Through dealings with different vendors, I firmly believe that the industry is beginning to realize that the largest constraint on future sales will be the lack of effectiveness of existing customer computer installations.

How can the vendor sell more hardware, if the existing equipment is not being utilized because we cannot build applications quickly enough? We see special software products being developed in an attempt to make computer systems more productive with less programming required. There are devices and programs to help support the programming staff so they can accomplish more. In almost every instance I recommend that the firm consider acquiring such devices and programs or at least evaluate them carefully. Here the vendor's interest is compatible with our own: to obtain greater effectiveness from the computer.

The instance in which I have difficulty with the advice of the vendor is when free consulting is offered to solve a problem. I am not sure that the vendor's need to sell equipment makes it possible to offer objective advice in the customer's best interest. One major computer manufacturer has a significant program of working with clients to develop a long-range plan for information systems. I fear that, with the pressure to sell equipment and services, this plan will not consider the full range of opportunities open to the customer. In this instance, I recommend the use of outside consultants if management needs assistance in developing a plan.

On balance, then, we want to have harmonious relations with the vendor. We shall obtain the most from the relationship if we critically evaluate the advice of the vendor and accept recommendations which are clearly in our best interest. If there is doubt, then seek external assistance. Remember, the management of the firm is ultimately responsible for its information-processing effort.

CHAPTER 10

What's an Application, Anyway?

IN PRIOR CHAPTERS we have talked informally about computer applications and discussed several examples; we relied on an informal and intuitive understanding of a computer application. Now it is time for a discussion of systems analysis and design, so a more formal definition of an application is needed.

A Definition

An "application" is a set of human and computer-based procedures that accomplish a given task. This definition stresses the fact that a computer application is a combination of human and machine-aided functions, a fact which is sometimes forgotten. The performance of individuals is necessary for a system to work.

This definition also indicates that the application is supposed to accomplish some task; the nature of this task usually identifies the application, like accounts receivable or inventory control. An application consists of human and machine procedures which are usually devoted to the processing of information for some particular business function.

If this is an application, what is a system? If you feel that the definition of an application is imprecise, you will probably find the definition of a system even worse. A system is sometimes defined in exactly the same way we have defined an application! (The term system is also used to describe a particular configuration of equipment which constitutes a computer system.)

For example, consider the national transportation system. This large system is made up of a number of subsystems such as surface and air travel subsystems. We can break surface travel into several components including highway, rail, and water. Similarly air travel can be broken into a series of subsystems like major and commuter carriers.

Generally, when we deal with a computer, we find that an application is identical with a subsystem. The subsystem is a component of all of the business systems in the firm. Since the terminology is used loosely, an application is often referred to as a system and the process of developing an application as systems analysis and design.

An Example

The semantics are a bit confusing, but the notion of an application is critical to understanding the role of computers in the firm. Consider the example in Figure 10–1. This is a simple block diagram of the processing required to enter an order for a hypothetical manufacturing company. In its present form the diagram could refer to a manual or a computer-based process. The diagram depicts orders which must be recorded by the firm; reports are produced for the sales function and for production while the orders themselves are filed.

Figure 10–2 represents the system in Figure 10–1 in more detail; now we see that this is in fact a computer application. An order is received and opened. For control purposes, a clerk enters the order number in a log. The clerk edits the orders, for example, by adding up the total number of units ordered and writing it on the bottom. The order then goes to an operator working at a terminal which is connected on-line to a computer.

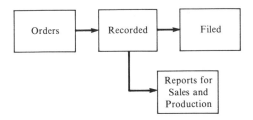

FIGURE 10-1   **Order Entry Example**

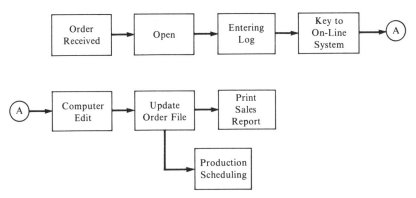

FIGURE 10-2   **More Details on Order Entry**

The operator enters the order and the computer responds with edits. For example, the operator keys in the order number and the computer displays the name and address of the customer. If they do not match the name and address on the order, there is a mistake and the operator must rectify it. The computer adds up all of the pieces ordered and compares the total with that computed by the clerk (also keyed by the terminal operator); a discrepancy is a sign that the order has been entered incorrectly. The computer updates a series of files containing open orders and prints a sales report. The application also includes a report for the production scheduling function.

We can view this application as one that encompasses order entry. Though primarily concerned with orders, the system does provide some information for other functions, sales and production. We might find upon closer examination that this system really has two subsystems or two applications. For example, the box for production scheduling in Figure 10–2 could be a great deal more involved. The order-entry application may feed data to production scheduling, an application that examines all pending requirements, matches them with inventory, and attempts to schedule production in a factory.

In this expanded application, we have integrated two subsystems: the data for production control is dependent on the order-entry application. The two applications may have been designed as subsystems of the same project or they may have been developed at completely separate points in time and then integrated.

The Portfolio

In the example above, we have more than one application, though both are closely related. An organization, then, has a series of applications that may be in various stages of development and use. This set constitutes a firm's applications portfolio.

Different applications employ different technology and are the primary responsibility of different groups of users. In fact, very few individuals in the firm may realize the full extent to which different operations are supported by computer applications.

The identification and selection of applications is a key part of management's role in controlling information processing. It is the demand for new applications and for creative uses of the technology that generates increasing requests for computer staff members and computer hardware. The type of applications developed and the technology employed determine the benefits the firm will achieve from its investment in computing.

Some Distinctions

How does the notion of a computer application fit with the trends in the industry toward personal computers, decision support systems, and so forth? We can examine different uses of computers, such as the following:

Game playing

Computing

Personal decision support systems

Applications

As we move down this list, we come closer to applications as we have defined them in this chapter.

Game playing is really not a very interesting application from an information-processing standpoint. Certainly it is entertaining, but the task is pure pleasure rather than the accomplishment of some organizational objective.

Next we find computing, which may seem a bit confusing because we have supposedly been talking about computing. Here I must use the word in a special context. "Computing" is what we do in universities and what your engineering staff may do if it uses a computer. It is also what the typical grade school or secondary school does: the computer is used as a calculating device. Most of the time, the person operating a terminal is the one who has the problem to be solved plus control of his or her own data. In an organization, this kind of computing is likely to be done by a staff member who may utilize an outside time-sharing computer rather than the firm's own machine.

Why isn't computing a computer application? Some types of computing approach the realm of applications, but for the most part they differ from applications because of the scale and the number of people involved. For example, a personal decision system developed for a small number of managers on a time-sharing computer is between straight computing and a major application. This personal system is not carefully coded to check for errors and does not access a large data base due to the nature of the problem being solved and the users involved.

Most computer applications are run repeatedly; the order-entry application is executed all day long. The typical computer application involves manual procedures and a number of individuals; it is most often developed by professional staff members to be used by others in the firm. This kind of application has to be concerned with data processing, editing, the distribution of reports, the maintenance of files, and so on.

When I encounter students reporting extensive experience with systems, the key question is whether they have actually worked on an application or have just been involved in computing. Some experts in the field suggest that the future for systems is bright because all of our future managers will be exposed to computers by the time they leave high school. Unfortunately, I fear that, like my students, they will be exposed to computing but will have little or no idea of how a computer application functions in an organization. They will fail to appreciate the large number of individuals involved, the scope of the project, the fact that the system is developed by professionals for others to use, and the fact that a computer application exists in a rich organizational context.

Summary

A typical computer application exists in an organization; it involves a combination of manual, human procedures and computer programs. The application is often developed by a group of computer professionals who design it to be operated by other individuals in the firm. As a result, a great deal of attention is paid to editing and error correction. Finally, the analyst is concerned with how this application fits with other applications that already exist.

The development of computer applications is a very important and difficult task for the organization. We shall explore this activity in more detail in the next few chapters.

CHAPTER 11

How Do You Justify a System?

THE TYPICAL ORGANIZATION, as we have seen, has a large number of computer applications. How has it made the decision to develop each one? When a system is suggested, the computer staff usually undertakes a feasibility study. This study describes the present system and its problems and sketches a possible design for a new, usually computer-based alternative. Users, managers, and the computer staff then decide whether to undertake the system.

In this chapter, we assume that the area in which the application has been suggested is now a part of an overall plan for information systems in the firm. Now we have reached the point of determining whether or not to undertake a specific application within the area. For example, if order processing is a high-priority applications area, our first task may be to consider what kind of an order entry system to develop, if any.

The Textbook Approach

The basis for determining the feasibility of an application is the cost-benefit study; at least that is what we advocate in textbooks.

The computer staff estimates the costs of a system while users and the staff estimate the benefits.

The cost-benefit approach is good for certain types of systems, those at the transactions-processing or operational-control level. With these systems we can usually find cost savings or the elimination of future costs to demonstrate. For example, a transactions-processing system may make it possible to expand the volume of transactions handled without incurring a proportionate increase in the number of employees. An inventory-control system may reduce inventory balances while holding service levels constant or even improving them.

Some Problems

Unfortunately, systems are designed for purposes other than pure cost savings, which makes a cost-benefit analysis difficult to complete. For systems in the managerial control and strategic planning categories, the user is often interested in better control, better decisions, or more relevant information. How does one assign a benefit in terms of dollars to such systems?

In many areas the manager makes decisions that are not based on costs and benefits. For some reason, the computer field has come to the conclusion that it exists to save money and, therefore, the only way to justify an application is to show cost savings. Of course, we always find a way to include intangible benefits, which makes it easy to manipulate the total benefits to create the appearance that a system has a payoff to the firm.

The Current Environment

In the present information-processing environment, we face a situation which is somewhat different from the one above. Rarely are we concerned with a single application in isolation. Rarely, given the power of the hardware, do we have an application suggested which is totally infeasible in any form. The real decision problem is (1) to select an appropriate alternative for an application and (2) to assign a priority to the alternative and to decide when it can be developed.

This situation arises because we have a very powerful technology, and our critical resource is the ability to design and program a system. The organization typically has a large backlog of applications that have been suggested; the task is to allocate scarce manpower to implement these desired applications.

The idea of forgoing the typical cost-benefit analysis should not be too shocking. There are many business decisions that are made without a cost-benefit analysis or calculations that show a monetary return. How is the advertising budget set? Does the typical firm try to show a dollar benefit from its research and development activities or, more to the point, for each project undertaken in an R&D lab?

Alternatives

I have read a number of feasibility studies for computer applications and have found remarkable similarities among them. Typically, they begin with a discussion of present information-processing procedures and then present a description of a new computer-based system to solve all of the problems of the existing system. Occasionally there will be a short appendix showing the alternatives for a new system that were rejected by the computer staff who performed the study.

Such a document places the manager in a difficult position. One has essentially the choice of taking or leaving the new system; there are no alternatives. Quite often, we would be happy with a system that did a little less than solve all of our problems.

For years, the automobile manufacturers have offered us a number of alternative ways to solve our transportation problems. We have a range of choices, from very small, economical cars to quite expensive luxury automobiles. A salesman driving 50,000 miles per year may want a large, luxury car while an executive commuting three miles to a train station may desire a small, economical car that is easy to park. Each of these individuals is in a different situation.

For a computer application, the customer (user) likewise should have some range of choices. We should insist upon presentation of a series of alternatives for a given application; then we can choose the alternative that is most appealing and assign a priority to it.

Consider our example in the last chapter. We presented a simple order-entry system and indicated that it might work with a production-scheduling and control system. What if the only proposal from the computer staff were the development of an integrated order-entry and production-scheduling system? While desirable, such a large system would take a long time to develop and would be quite expensive.

It would be more helpful to have a range of alternatives presented. We could look at several order-entry possibilities alone, such as an on-line system using paper orders, an on-line system using operators with keyboards to whom salesmen phone their orders, or a package program that would be modified and installed at our firm. The same alternatives could be explored for the production-scheduling and control application.

Evaluation

One of the problems confronting managers is the lack of consistent criteria on which new applications are approved. One application is selected for cost savings, another for the marketing department because they haven't had a system in a while, and so on. I recommend that the users and the computer staff develop a list of criteria for evaluating each alternative for a given application. The criteria should be used as consistently as possible regarding different applications so that we can compare the reasons for adopting one application with the reasons for adopting or rejecting another.

Examples of possible criteria include:

Percentage of user needs met

Cost to develop

Cost to operate

Length of time to develop

Cost savings

Operational improvements

Information improvements

Contribution to revenue

There are obviously more criteria; each company should develop its own list. Probably no more than seven to ten criteria should be specified since too much information may complicate the decision.

If one wishes this process to be a little more sophisticated, each alternative to an application can be rated on the list of criteria and then scored. In fact, we can even weight the various criteria so that particular ones exert more influence on the score than do others.

A Mechanism

The main objective of the above approach is to provide well-structured information for users and managers to use in deciding which alternative to select for a given application. The insistence on multiple alternatives means that there will really be a decision. Using some set of criteria insures that all of the alternatives will be evaluated on the same basis.

But what kind of mechanism is there for making the final choice and, more important, assigning a priority to it? For this purpose, I advocate an applications selection committee. The users most likely to be involved with a specific system should have the primary input on the alternative to be chosen for a particular application. However, as we mentioned earlier, it is unlikely that work can begin immediately on a new system. Instead, a larger committee representing users from different functional areas in the firm and the computer staff must meet to assign priorities.

This committee must remain aware of applications currently under development and those which have been approved but are waiting for development. The committee should have a great deal of freedom in adjusting the priorities and schedules of projects that have yet to be undertaken. An important system can be moved to the front of the queue; a less important system may not be scheduled for development for a relatively long time.

There must be some flexibility for the committee to take resources from present applications, but it should be limited. The problem with the concept of a portfolio of applications is that there is no market for the contents of the portfolio, at least for the ones under development. Thus, we can cancel a project and assign the resources elsewhere; but this is a fairly drastic step and is not generally taken unless business conditions change dramatically or a project is found to be infeasible after it is started.

More realistically, we can reduce the resources assigned to a project and thus stretch out its development time. The freed resources, usually in the form of manpower, can be assigned to a higher priority project. Often we will do this to meet a critical application that must be finished in a short period of time. Perhaps a government report is required, a change in business conditions means that we must alter our order-entry system, or some similar change is needed on a crucial system.

One can also think of adding resources to a project that is behind schedule or whose priority is raised. However, depending on the stage of development, there are limits to what can be accomplished with additional people assigned to a computer development project. Unless subsystems or pieces of the design task can be separated from the entire project, it can sometimes be counterproductive to increase the size of a staff. New staff members have to learn what has been done so far and must be given tasks they can complete. Project management must be consulted to determine whether added manpower will in fact make a positive contribution, given the stage of development of a particular system.

Summary

In this chapter we have tried to offer an alternative to the traditional ways in which systems are justified. A focus on cost savings may lead us to develop systems that miss the potential of the computer to increase revenues or improve decision making.

Our objective has been to provide a mechanism and information structure for the decision of which application to undertake. I argued that the question is usually not one of feasibility but, rather, one of which alternative for a particular application is best suited to our needs. Users of the system, with help from the computer staff, are in the best position to make this decision.

Once an alternative has been selected, then a group of users and managers representing a general overview of the entire firm are in a position to assign a priority to the application. This group can take into account the competing objectives and the needs of different areas within the company.

The results of this approach to project justification and selection should be greater satisfaction with the process and the development of applications according to their priority for the firm.

CHAPTER 12

How Do We Design a System?

THE DESIGN OF an information system is a creative, intellectual task. The work is similar to that of any design project, like an architect planning a new building. First we form a rough sketch of a concept for the building. The architect provides several elevations showing different views and a floor plan. We modify the plans and go through several review and revisions cycles; finally the specifications are developed in detail and construction actually begins. During the construction we may see problems and make some modifications to the original specifications. Finally, the project is completed; further activities involve maintenance or improvements in the form of remodeling.

In the case of an information system we do much the same thing. The problem with a system, however, is its lack of concrete substance. We all have experience as users of buildings. An architect's plan is quite descriptive; it is easy to picture the exterior of a building from the drawings. If this is not sufficient, the designer often reverts to a model of wood or cardboard.

As in the building analogy, it is important to begin with a good design for the structure of a computer application because changes are more costly as development proceeds. To change a room size on the first sketches is easy; during construction, the change is much more costly and difficult. The same is true of the information system. During the initial design stages changes are simple; later, during programming and testing, they become more difficult and costly.

The Systems Life Cycle

A computer-based information system has a life cycle, just like a living organism or a new product. The various stages in the life of a system are shown in Table 12-1. The idea for a new information system is stimulated by a need to improve information-processing procedures. This need leads to the preliminary survey to determine whether a system can be developed to solve these processing problems. If the results of the survey are positive, they are refined to produce a more detailed feasibility study. Based on the outcome of the feasibility study, the decision whether to proceed with the design of a system is made. One of the alternatives sketched in the feasibility study is chosen for development if the decision is positive.

In systems analysis, existing information-processing procedures are documented in detail. One major task during this phase is to define the boundaries of the system. Does the problem concern just inventory control, or should any new system also consider the problems in purchasing when inventory has to be replenished? During analysis, data on the volume of transactions, decision points, and existing files are also collected.

The most challenging and creative part of the life cycle is the design of a new system. One way to approach this task is to develop an ideal system which is relatively unconstrained by cost or technology; this ideal system is then refined until it becomes feasible. Detailed specifications must be prepared for the system just designed. The exact logic to be followed in processing and the contents and structure of the files must be specified. Input and output (I/O) devices are selected, and the formats for I/O are developed. These requirements for processing, files, and I/O ac-

TABLE 12-1   The Systems Life Cycle

Inception
  Preliminary survey
Feasibility Study
  Existing procedures
  Alternative systems
  Cost estimates
Systems Analysis
  Details of present procedures
  Collection of data on volumes, input/output, files
Design
  Ideal system unconstrained
  Revisions to make ideal feasible
Specifications
  Processing logic
  File design
  Input/output
  Programming requirements
  Manual procedures
Programming
Testing
  Unit tests
  Combined module tests
  Acceptance tests
Training
Conversion and Installation
Operations
  Maintenance
  Enhancements

SOURCE: From *The Analysis, Design, and Implementation of Information Systems,* 2 ed., by Henry C. Lucas, Jr. Copyright © 1981, 1976, by McGraw-Hill, Inc. Used [as edited] with the permission of McGraw-Hill Book Co.

tivities lead to the specification of programming requirements; these requirements can be turned over to a programming staff for coding.

In the programming stage, the actual computer programs necessary to perform the logic operations of processing are written. In some organizations this task is done by a separate group of programmers, while other organizations use analyst-programmers. The same individuals who perform the systems analysis and design also code the resulting programs. Programs have to be tested carefully, first as units and then in combined modules. Usually a programming task is broken down into a series of smaller subtasks or modules; all of the individual modules must operate together if the system is to work properly. During the final stages of testing, there will be some type of acceptance test in which users verify that the system works satisfactorily.

Since one purpose of the new information-processing system is to change existing procedures, training is crucial. All individuals have to understand what is required by the new system. When training has been completed, it is possible to undertake conversion; it may be necessary to write special programs to convert existing files into new ones or to create files from manual records. Finally, after all these stages, the system is installed.

After the problems of installation have been resolved and the organization has adjusted to the changes created by the new system, the operational stage is begun; that is, the system now operates on a routine basis. However, this does not mean that it remains unchanged; there is a constant need for maintenance and enhancements. Maintenance is required because programs inevitably have errors which must be corrected when they appear. Because of the creative nature of design, users and the computer staff may not have communicated accurately, so that certain aspects of the system must be modified as operational experience is gained with it. As users work with the system, they will learn more about it and will develop ideas for change and enhancements. It is unreasonable to consider a computer-based information system finished; the system continues to evolve throughout its life cycle if, in fact, it is successful.

Figure 12–1 shows the resources required during each stage of the life cycle of a typical system. The pattern of time required would be much the same. Very few resources are usually needed during the inception and feasibility study. Once systems analysis is begun, more expenses will be incurred as analysts and users work on the system and its design. These stages culminate in the preparation of specifications from which programming can begin.

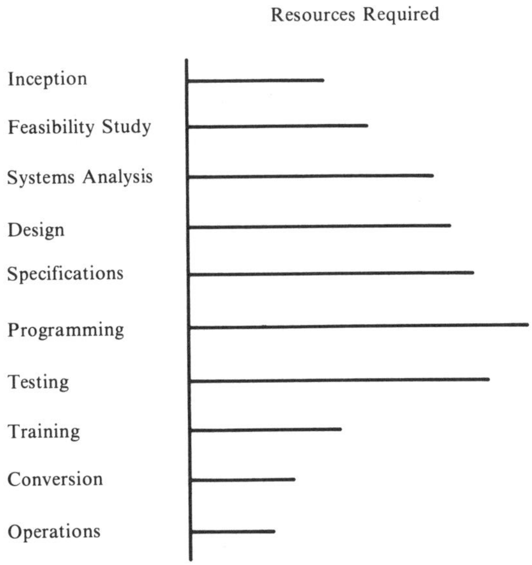

Resources Required

Inception	
Feasibility Study	
Systems Analysis	
Design	
Specifications	
Programming	
Testing	
Training	
Conversion	
Operations	

FIGURE 12–1 **Typical Resource Requirements During Systems Anal-
ysis and Design**

The programming stage is intensive and requires the most resources. For a large project, the entire process of design can last two years or more—of which more than a year may be required to write and test programs. Training is concurrent with the later stages of programming; finally, the system will be converted and installed. After this time, the system reverts to operational status and is run on a routine basis. The resources required here are steady, with some increases as the system becomes older and more changes are requested.

One major trend in the industry is a movement of the design process forward, that is, spending more time in analysis and design. If a system is better specified, there are fewer changes during programming; these changes often require major redesign of programs and files, a very costly process. Through careful design, we can drastically reduce subsequent problems with the application.

Responsibilities During the Life Cycle

Users, management, and the information services department staff interact in a number of ways during the analysis, design, and operation of information systems. Because this task is so complex and demanding, it is essential that all three groups cooperate during the analysis and design process. Table 12–2 restates the stages in the systems life cycle and suggests the appropriate roles for users, management, and the information services department.

The user initiates the preliminary survey by suggesting a potential application. The information services department responds with a rough estimate of its desirability and with several alternative systems, for example, improvements to present information-processing activities, a batch system, a package, or even an on-line system, each meeting some percentage of user needs. Management must approve the basic suggestion and the idea of a new computer application in this area of the firm; management should also participate in setting the objectives for any new system. A preliminary survey evaluates each alternative with criteria developed by a steering committee. The steering committee, with management participation, authorizes a feasibility study, possibly eliminating some alternatives suggested in the preliminary survey.

The information services department staff conducts the feasibility study with help and advice from users. Users conduct an analysis of the existing system and help the information services department evaluate various alternatives, using the criteria specified by the steering committee. Management reviews the feasibility of the proposed alternatives and develops an understanding of what the system will accomplish. The steering committee, with participation and review by management, selects the alternative for implementation. Should the committee choose the alternative of no new system, the application may be held in abeyance until changing conditions make it feasible.

If the decision is to proceed with the development of a new system, users and the information services department staff collaborate to analyze the existing system. Users aid by explaining existing processing procedures and by providing data. The computer staff uses this information to document the existing system and to help establish the boundaries of a new system. Management has a key role to play in this stage; it must provide adequate resources for both the information services department and for users. It may be necessary to hire additional staff so that users can participate or to hire additional analysts to work on the project.

Next the design of a new system begins; I advocate that users design their own input, output, and basic processing logic. The information services department acts as a catalyst, presenting alternatives for users to consider. Management encourages user design through its own attendance at review meetings. Management may provide special rewards, prizes, or other incentives to help encourage user participation in design. Management also must plan for the impact of the system on the organization at this point. Will the structure of the organization be changed? How will work groups be affected? What will specific individuals do as a result of the system? A plan for conversion, including a forecast of the impact of the system on all potential users, should be developed. A conversion plan can be started at this point and users can work on the design of any manual procedures associated with the new system.

The information services staff develops detailed specifications based on the logic and requirements specified by users; the staff also prepares a technical conversion plan. The users on the design team review the technical plans and also work on the development of specifications for manual procedures. It is vitally important at this stage for both users and managers to understand the system. Users must be familiar with the input, output and processing logic. Management must understand the overall flow of the system and be aware of key decisions. For example, management should be aware if inventory items are to be grouped into classes with different reordering rules applied to each class. Management should help set the classification and reorder rules and understand how the logic is to work.

The user and management role during programming is one of monitoring progress. Are modern techniques being used to

TABLE 12-2 Responsibilities During the System Life Cycle

STAGES	RESPONSIBILITIES OF		
	Users	Management	Information-Services Staff
Inception	Initiate study, suggest application, sketch information needs, describe existing processing procedures	Approve area for application, set objectives	Listen to requirements, respond to questions, devise alternatives, assess using rough estimates, prepare preliminary survey
Feasibility Study	Help evaluate existing system and proposed alternatives, select alternative for design	Review feasibility, understand proposals, choose alternative	Evaluate alternatives using agreed-upon criteria
Systems Analysis	Help describe existing system, collect and analyze data	Provide resources, attend reviews	Conduct analysis, collect data, document findings
Design	Design input/output and processing logic, plan for conversion and forecast impact on users, design manual procedures, remain aware of file structures and design	Encourage user design, provide rewards, attend reviews, plan impact	Present alternatives and tradeoffs to users for their decisions

Specifications	Review specifications, help develop specifications for manual procedures	Understand high level logic and key features	Combine user needs with technical requirements to develop specifications, develop technical conversion plan
Programming	Monitor progress	Monitor, provide buffer and extra resources	Organize programming, design modules, code programs, report progress
Testing	Generate test data, evaluate results	Review	Test program modules individually and in entire system
Training	Develop materials, conduct training sessions	Review	Aid in preparation of materials, train operations staff
Conversion and Installation	Phase conversion, provide resources, conduct post-implementation audit	Attend user sessions, demonstrate own commitment	Coordinate conversion, perform conversion processing tasks, help in post-implementation audit
Operations	Provide data, utilize output, monitor system use and quality, suggest modifications and enhancements	Monitor	Process data to produce output reliability, respond to enhancement requests, suggest improvements, monitor service

Source: From *Information Systems Concepts for Management*, 2 ed., by Henry C. Lucas, Jr. Copyright © 1982, 1978 by McGraw-Hill, Inc. Used [as edited] with the permission of McGraw-Hill Book Co.

manage programming? Is a project schedule maintained and are resources reallocated as necessary to achieve installation on schedule? The bulk of the responsibility during this design stage rests with the information services department. The staff must design program modules, code them, and test them both alone and in combination. Management should realize the importance of their involvement and assistance when problems arise. The development of a computer-based system is similar to a research and development project; it is very difficult to anticipate every contingency. There will be project slippages, budget overruns, and other problems. The role of management is to provide a buffer for the project and to furnish additional resources where they will help.

During testing, users should define data for test programs and attempt to generate data with errors to ascertain whether the system will catch them. Users should carefully examine test results and evaluate the adequacy of processing; management should also participate in the reviews of data processed by the system. Some kind of acceptance test should be conducted by the information services department and its results evaluated by users; a parallel test of old and new procedures or pilot studies may be used for this purpose.

A training period is essential for smooth conversion and installation. Users develop materials and actually conduct the training sessions. Management remains aware of the training program, attends occasional sessions to communicate support for the system, and checks that its knowledge of the system is accurate. Training can often be combined with testing since preparation of test data serves to help train users. The information services staff aids in the preparation of materials and has the responsibility of training the operations staff.

Conversion is a crucial part of the systems life cycle; it should be phased if it is possible to select one department or geographic area to be converted first. The information services department coordinates conversion and performs conversion procedures such as creating initial files for the new system. Users and the information services department should jointly conduct a post-implementation audit and report the results to management. How well does the system meet specifications? How good were the specifications; that it, how do users react to the system now? How do the original estimates compare with what was achieved? These data can be helpful in making estimates for future projects.

Finally, during operations, users furnish data for input and work with the output. Users and management will probably suggest enhancements and modifications to the system over time. The information services department should also look for potential improvements and respond to modifications suggested by users.

Summary

Systems analysis and design is an exciting and creative activity. It is also very time-consuming, expensive, and frequently frustrating. If we pay insufficient attention to the task, we end up with a system that is unusable or clumsy. Many systems have failed because of insufficient user understanding and input in the design process.

This chapter has presented only an overview of the complicated task of analysis and design. A major system can take one to three years to design and install and can easily cost hundreds of thousands of dollars. We are working on ways to reduce the length of time required to produce systems, but it appears unlikely that we shall automate the entire design task. I expect that these new tools will facilitate design by making it easier to develop prototypes, but we still must decide what kind of system we want, what information is to be processed, and how it will be processed. Even with advanced tools, we will still have to undertake systems analysis and design. Firms where managers, users, and the computer staff cooperate and perform their roles in design should be the most successful in this process.

CHAPTER 13

Why Do Good Systems Fail?

IT IS ONE OF THE TRAGEDIES of the information systems profession that so many seemingly well-conceived systems end up as failures. By a failure I mean a system that does not come close to its potential, to original design objectives, or does not ever work at all. Many of these systems are still run, but no one really cares whether they exist or not.

Because systems development is such a complex task, there are many opportunities for errors. If ever Murphy's law—"whenever something can go wrong, it will"—applied, it does in information processing. In fact, it has been suggested that, in regard to computers, Murphy was an optimist!

In the inception stage, it is very easy to develop unrealistic objectives for a system and unrealistic expectations for what the system will do. In the feasibility study we are looking at the tip of the iceberg; it is too expensive to delve into all details of the system at this point. We make informed estimates (guesses) and hope that we are right in forecasting cost, time, and what can be accomplished.

In systems analysis, we typically omit crucial parts of the design because it is such a difficult task to anticipate all requirements for a system. As a result, the specifications for the system are incomplete and often contradictory. Remember, we have taken a lot of different views of the information system and data and molded them into a single picture of a system; there are bound to be errors in this process.

We have also found the task of converting specifications into programs to be a difficult one. Programming, though rapidly improving, has a research and development flavor to it. Even a simple system can require complex programming. For an on-line transactions-processing system, for example, 60 to 80 percent of the program may be devoted to checking for and recovering from user input errors or errors in the data.

If we fail to test a program adequately with sample data, real data, and tests at high levels of volume, we run the risk of missing major errors that the testing process is supposed to detect. In fact, even if we want to, it would be impossible to test every path in the program with data because there are just too many different routes through a program. As a result, no program is ever fully debugged or 100 percent correct, a reason for some of the maintenance we incur when the system is operational.

If we fail to train users properly or to anticipate the impact of the system on them, we may run into significant conversion and installation problems. Once installed, we operate the system; we gradually find the design and programming errors as the system is used. Some preliminary statistics indicate that well over half of the errors found are those made in design; many fewer are programming bugs.

Given all of these possibilities, maybe we should be amazed that a system ever works, not that so many fail!

The Greatest Failings

Organizational Problems

Among all of the problems already listed, probably the most consistent reason for failure in the field has been the failure to consider the impact of the implementation process itself. We design an information system to change existing information-processing procedures; every system therefore creates change. The change may be quite simple; an individual may work with a new terminal, input form, or output report. However, the change may also be quite dramatic, with new work groups or even whole new departments created.

The failure to consider the impact of a proposed system on the organization and on individuals has resulted in a significant number of problems with systems. Individuals refuse to provide input, work against the development of the system, and fail to use the output. As a result, a large investment is partially wasted.

All during the design process, it is important to motivate users to help in the design of a system and eventually to use the system once it is available. This means that users must see some benefit to themselves from the system; they must also see that their work on the development of the system will help them to attain these benefits.

In too many instances, no attention has been paid to this human aspect of the design process. Sometimes management even uses a system as a vehicle to institute unpopular changes in the organization. One firm wanted to unify customer services and to remove this function from the two departments currently serving customers. Instead of presenting the formation of a single, new department as a management objective, executives took the easy way of commissioning a computer system and making the change a part of the installation of the system. The flaw in this strategy was that the change was highly unpopular; users working on the system kept trying to influence it so that the change would not occur. When management made clear in a system review meeting that the organizational change was independent of the system, the design team could focus its attention on the objective of developing a system to work with a new organizational structure.

Examine carefully the changes that a system will create. Are you asking one group in the organization to bear all of the costs of using the system, for example, to provide all of the input? Does this group who pays the cost receive any benefits or do all of the advantages of the system accrue to different users? If there are no benefits, can we provide some incentives to use the system? Are changes carefully analyzed, and does management know its own objectives for the structure of the organization and work groups?

Technical Problems

There are other reasons why systems fail besides these dealing with organizational and personal factors. Many of the other reasons are technical; perhaps the application is totally unprecedented and it is just not possible to do what was envisioned in the original specifications. As each part of the system is developed, we begin to see more of the iceberg, to understand how much effort remains. There are managers of information services departments who will commit to estimates only for the next phase of a project and who divide a project into from five to fifteen stages. They ask their staff to hit their estimates for development cost and time within 20 percent at each stage.

Project Management Problems

Frequently projects seem to be developing well but then fall behind schedule; costs begin to exceed the budget and critical milestones are missed. To recover lost time and save money, the system is scaled back so that less is delivered than was promised. In more than one case, late systems have been installed after inadequate testing—and the results have been chaotic for users and the firm.

As we mentioned in the last chapter, senior management must monitor progress on the application to be sure that the information services department staff is functioning properly. Are they using some kind of management technique to monitor progress? For example, there are critical path techniques that have been adopted from other kinds of projects. There are also special systems and life cycle methodologies that assist in following the course of a project.

The next task of management is to know what to do if the project is not proceeding well. In some instances, it is probably permissible to think about replacing people and making an issue out of the delay. However, there are other times when the best action is to add resources or to consider slowing the project down. It is a difficult task to know which action is appropriate; the manager must understand what is responsible for the problem and determine whether more resources are warranted. Adding staff is not always the answer; a new employee may not be able to catch up with the others who are deep in the development of the system.

Summary

There is no one reason why information systems fail. Three broad categories of significant problems do emerge, however: organizational, technical, and managerial. By carefully considering the impact of a system on the organization and on individuals during the design process, we can reduce the potential for implementation problems. To keep control over the project and its possible technical difficulties, it is necessary to have a good project management arrangement. Management must monitor these aspects of systems development and be prepared to take appropriate action in order to increase the probability of a successful system.

CHAPTER 14

Why Get Involved?

FOR A NUMBER OF YEARS I have argued that managers and users need to become more involved in the development and management of information systems. In this chapter, I try to summarize some of the main reasons for my belief that this involvement is essential in gaining control of information processing.

Some of the major reasons for high levels of involvement in design are:

1. When a system is installed, it is used by managers and others, not the computer department staff that developed it. It is important for the end user to understand the features of the system and to influence its development since that individual, not the developers, will be living with it.

2. Heavy participation in systems design means that the user is more knowledgeable about the final system and requires less training.

3. The user has the in-depth knowledge necessary to design a system. It is unrealistic to expect the systems analyst to be

expert in all aspects of the business as well as in information-processing technology.

4. There are a number of decisions which have to be made about information systems that involve user and business considerations; it is virtually impossible for a professional computer-staff member to make these decisions in isolation from users and management.

Today, in addition to the reasons above, we are faced with a whole new set of problems which increases the importance of manager and user involvement in computing activities: there are not enough computer professionals to develop all the applications we desire.

The People Gap

We have abundant and relatively inexpensive computer hardware; the serious bottleneck in the field is the availability of skilled computer personnel to cope with the large demand for new systems. There is a dramatic shortage of both systems analysts and programmers. One source estimates that we are short 10 percent of the number of programmers that we need and that, by 1990, we will need to triple the number of these individuals to reach a total of 1.5 million. It is highly unlikely that such a growth level will be achieved.

In most organizations I have encountered, there is a large backlog of requests for new applications and for maintenance and enhancements to existing systems. Maintenance is necessary to repair problems found within systems, errors in the original coding that were not caught in testing and features of the design that are not operating smoothly. Enhancements represent changes to a system to improve its usefulness to users; examples would include a new report, the addition of new data to a file, and similar changes. I recently visited a company with a $4 million budget for computing. At the end of the month of my visit they had 132 change requests that would require approximately 7,000 man-hours to complete.

As we mentioned earlier, surveys have suggested that the average firm spends about 50 percent of its budget for systems work on maintenance and enhancements. However, in some organizations the rate for maintenance and enhancements is as high as 85 percent, meaning that there is very little budget left for the development of new systems.

The combination of maintenance and enhancements requiring so many resources and of the exploding user demand for new systems explains the large backlog of new applications. One study found that users had many applications in planning, waiting for the computer staff to have time to undertake them. In addition, these users had about the same number of applications which they had not yet suggested because they were discouraged by the existing backlog.

We can add to the reasons for greater user and manager involvement in systems the compelling reason that *there are not enough professionals to develop and maintain systems.* In order to obtain results from computer-based information systems, all individuals in the organization, not just the computer staff, will have to work on systems.

Systems Analysis and Design

Users

Users should be heavily involved in the initiation of a new system. They must help sketch the new system and assist in the decision as to whether the development of a new application is feasible and desirable. Users can and should be heavily involved in the actual design of a system; I have had some success using a systems design team headed by a user.

The user must be interested in the system and take the initiative. He or she works closely with the analyst in charge of the project for the information services department. The analyst acts as a tour guide, explaining the various stages of design and presenting major decision and trade-offs to the design team. The design team might consist of five or ten users and two to five analysts, depending on the size of the system being developed.

The design team meets as a whole and in various subgroups to carry out the tasks assigned to the smaller subgroups. A significant part of this design process is the group review or walk-through of the logic of the system. In the beginning, the design reviews concentrate on the concepts of the system. It is very important for senior level managers to be included in these review meetings because they may often have important policy input for the design. In one firm, senior management had clear ideas for the development of a unified forecast for sales and for the classification of inventory. The types of decisions being made could not be delegated to lower level employees in the firm; this might have happened if managers had remained aloof from the design process.

Later design meetings may focus on a small part of the system, such as the forecasting routine for a certain group of products. Appropriate levels of management should be included here, too. The review meetings may last from several hours to a day; however, many days of preparation by a large number of individuals precede each meeting. The manager does not have to commit much time other than that of the reviews themselves, so the time devoted to design by senior management can be kept to a reasonable amount.

Management

Management must provide resources so that users can play the role described above. This may involve hiring extra staff members to free users to participate in design. However, just providing resources is not enough; management must also participate in the design process.

Many systems are undertaken for a variety of objectives. In one instance, top management wanted to streamline customer services and move to a unified sales forecast which would be used by both marketing and production planning. However, these objectives were never clearly stated by management; they appeared to be a by-product of the design of the new computer system. The resulting unpopular changes caused a great deal of user resentment of the system.

When a review meeting was held and senior management presented its policy objectives, the users of the system began to realize that changes were not being made for the convenience of the system and that the changes were conscious and desired by management. This clear statement of management policy and objectives helped focus efforts on the design and removed much of the resentment users felt toward it.

Managers should also review the feasibility of proposed systems and examine different alternatives; management is the only group in a position to identify the key areas in which applications should be undertaken. Having made this decision, management should then provide adequate resources and attend review meetings.

Even seemingly simple systems often have implications for management policy. Consider, for example, a system to forecast sales and to set inventory reorder points. If the designers of the system suggest that inventory should be grouped into three classes such as fast moving, regular, and slow moving and that each class should be treated differently, there are significant implications for management. Management must first agree to the concept and then participate in setting the various reorder rules for the different classes. Systems like this have the potential for creating major changes in the way the business functions and, as such, become the responsibility of management.

Consistent management participation also sets an example; it indicates to others in the firm that management values information systems. It is surprising how much attention others in the organization pay to the subtle cues provided by management actions. If managers make an effort to understand a new system, attend review meetings, and participate in general in its development, they encourage others in the organization to make similar contributions. The results will be better systems having a greater chance of success.

Information Services Department

The role of the information services department is generally to act as a technical resource and guide in the development process. However, we should remember that *systems analysis and design is too important to be left entirely to the professional designer.* Instead, as described above, users and management must take charge of development efforts.

The systems analyst describes the various stages in the system life cycle and explains what has to be accomplished in each. The systems staff can also determine various alternatives for a specific system; they document the different designs that are developed.

During programming, the technical staff has the most activity. I do not expect users to write programs for a major new system. The professional designer also must help coordinate the conversion process for a new system and write any programs necessary for this task.

After the system has been installed, it is turned over to the operations staff for continued processing. At this point, the original designers from the computer department have finished their task. Generally, a different group will assume the responsibility for making changes to the system and correcting errors. The system now belongs to the user, whether he likes it or not!

Conclusion

There are many good reasons for managers and users to become closely involved in systems analysis and design. For the manager it is one way to gain more control over information processing; now the manager can help make key decisions, remain aware of progress on an application, and become more knowledgeable about the system. The user has an equally important role to play. The key management task is to ensure that all who should be involved in the development of a new system take the time and responsibility to do so.

CHAPTER 15

Why Can't Those #?*! Operate a Computer?

"WHY ARE THE REPORTS always late?" "Why does the on-line system have such terrible response?" "There are errors in everything we get."

Comments like those above are attributed to operations, the actual running of the computer center. Operations is not an easy job; there are many problems, a lot of pressure, and ceaseless deadlines that have to be met.

Batch Processing

In the early days of computing, there were no terminals; most input of data was via punched cards. A set of forms was gathered together in a batch (hence the name "batch processing") and keypunched. The keypunching was verified by having all of the input rekeyed on a separate machine that indicated when a keystroke differed from the hole punched in the card.

A computer program edited the batch for strange values or alphabetic data where there should be numbers. The computer also usually did a batch total on some figure in the input batch which was compared with the total entered on a batch control card computed by a clerk at an adding machine. If the totals matched, all of the input in that batch had been entered correctly.

The edited input updated historical records on a computer file and various output reports were produced. The reports were printed and then prepared for distribution. Since many copies of the report were printed with carbon paper between, the report had to be separated into copies and the pages split from the continuous form running through the printer.

Today, there are still many batch processing systems. There are fewer punched cards as they are replaced by other key input devices. A number of systems collect data on-line but update files at one point in time by using batches of input data.

For transactions-processing systems, there can be large numbers of individuals working with massive amounts of paper. Consider a bank processing checks. As the checks come in and are debited against the account, they have to be filed by account. When the monthly statements are run, the filed checks are retrieved and enclosed with the statements for mailing. It is no wonder that some of the credit-card companies have stopped sending sales slips; it is much easier to enter descriptive information about the purchase from a keyboard than to handle all of the pieces of paper for purchases.

There is often a control section that checks report totals before they are released. Programs have a number of error checks to insure that processing is done correctly. The clerks in the control section may, for example, check that the total payments from last month plus this month's transactions equal the new balance in an account.

Now what can go wrong in all of this? Why might reports have errors? I often hear complaints about incorrect sales reports which should be accurate since they are really the by-products of systems like order entry and shipping. There can be problems caused by operators, but there can also be input problems that originate with the user. A large order may be omitted because the salesman has not yet sent it in though he has notified sales management, so they are looking for it on the report. Even if the order was sent in, possibly it did not arrive before the cutoff for processing on a particular day.

There can be errors in sales reports that arise from the logic in a program. In one bank two different programs calculated a particular quantity and printed it on two different reports that were sent to branch managers. That number should have been the same on both reports, but it never was. Branch managers told me they disregarded almost all figures on both reports because of the consistent discrepancy between the two numbers.

The programs operated as they had been written. However, the calculations to arrive at that number differed in the two programs because different users had supplied the computer staff with different rules for calculating the results. In this case, the different users needed to meet with the computer staff to define a common set of rules. Unfortunately, users tended to blame computer operators for the problem.

It is not simply a matter of knowing who is at fault or where we have problems. One must track down errors, find the problem, and correct it. Too often errors are not resolved, and they create a great deal of user dissatisfaction.

On-line

On-line systems are more flexible and responsive to the user, if they work. With an on-line system, there may be batch reports as well as on-line data entry, inquiry, and updating. The appearance of an on-line computer operation is generally much more calm than that of batch processing. However, problems may still occur. Equipment can fail, or more likely, bugs in the system can cause problems. On-line systems are complex, particularly when telecommunications is involved. Any on-line system where the terminals are more than a mile or so from the computer requires the use of telephone lines. There can be failures and problems with any or all of this equipment.

For a critical on-line system like an airline reservations application, we generally find backup computers and complex communications networks with different routings available to act as a backup. A good technical staff is required to keep this system running well.

One chronic complaint about on-line processing is the problem of response time. Unfortunately, there is no agreement as to what constitutes acceptable response time; it depends on how long one is willing to sit at a terminal and wait for the computer to reply after a request is entered. A lot of factors influence response time, including the hardware, software, and the nature of the inquiry. For the most part, response times in the two-second range are great, three to six seconds tolerable, and more than eight or nine seconds irritating, depending on the application.

On-line computer systems, however, are not a great deal different from other user-oriented facilities. Mass transit experiences a peak when there may not be enough capacity; riders must stand rather than sit. Realistically, the cost of providing a seat for every passenger at every hour of the day would be prohibitive.

The situation is a little better in computing, but we still see wide fluctuations in the demand for processing during the day. Generally, we configure a system to provide good average response times under typical load and acceptable response under peak conditions. However, if the volume of transactions grows rapidly, then the system may not be able to maintain its pace and response times will degenerate. There is usually a simple solution: add more processing power; but most computer centers have been unable to satisfy all the demands on them and managers are wary of requesting more approvals for equipment.

Why can't we plan better? I guess the main reason is the unpredictability of users; demand seems to outstrip even our most extravagant estimates. As long as the transactions going through the on-line system are doing some good, then I am not terribly bothered by the need for more capacity. At least users are working with the system and find it important to their jobs.

Evaluation

Our objective is to instill an orientation toward service into the operations staff. Too often the demands and the pressures of the job tend to overshadow the reason the job is being done. One of the major problems I have with operations is the isolation most computer departments have from their users at this level.

I have been told a story about one computer center in Europe where the computer staff telephones a sample of users every afternoon in order to obtain constant feedback. The average of user satisfaction scores appears prominently on a lighted display in the computer room. Every computer operations employee focuses on that display as it changes during the day—the objective is to keep the satisfaction rating high. I do not know if such a center actually exists, but the idea is appealing.

The first part of emphasizing service is to know what level of service is being provided. Then operations management can concentrate on improving performance. Unfortunately, very few computer departments measure the real service they provide their users.

Even the departments that do measure their service often do it in a self-serving and meaningless way. One bank computer department developed 69 timeliness standards and over 129 quality indicators itself. It faithfully reported on all of these metrics to users every month. As a professor, this would be equivalent to letting me define and complete the student course evaluations at the end of the term, rating myself and the course!

Let me follow the above analogy a little further. We have developed a quite comprehensive course evaluation instrument at NYU that only takes about five minutes to complete at the end of the term. The first step in designing the instrument was to ask questions of students regarding what they considered facilitated learning. Perhaps 200 questions were on the first questionnaire. The responses were analyzed statistically, and questions that seemed to group together and be consistent were retained. After a number of tests and revisions, a short questionnaire resulted; it is printed on both sides of one sheet of paper.

There are 50 or 60 short questions to be answered Yes or No. These questions are analyzed statistically to extract five or six major factors which are reported to the faculty and published for students. An example of one of these factors would be "Instructor in Class," and a short explanation describes the components of the factor, such as good preparation and delivery.

I could not possibly figure out what to do with 60 or 70 individual questions, the type of system in use at some other schools. However, I can examine a few aggregate variables and then study their components in more detail to try to improve the quality of the class.

The same type of instrument could be developed for the operation of a computer center. Users could be asked to complete it on a quarterly basis or even monthly if there is a major improvement program under way. A few significant factors should indicate how operations are performing. Such a measure would be defined and completed by users and could be employed in conjunction with self-report measures from the computer department, such as the percentage of time the on-line system was available, the delivery of reports on schedule, and similar indicators.

At regular intervals, perhaps every six months, we can collect these user survey data and the indicators for the computer department. The progress of the department should be monitored over time. Management can take action, like offering a bonus when certain service-level objectives are achieved. If management emphasizes service, it can orient the operations staff to the importance of serving its customers. Through attention, rewards, and adequate resources we can enjoy successful operations.

CHAPTER 16

How Should We Charge for Computing?

MANAGERS EXPRESS A GREAT DEAL of interest in and frustration over the question of charging for computer services. I have heard strong emotional arguments regarding whether and how one might charge. The decision to charge and the mechanism for it depend primarily on one's objectives and the history of the organization.

Charging Methods

Two basic types of cost are associated with computer activities: development and operations. Development costs are incurred during the design of a new system. They can be estimated in advance, but our history has not been one of conspicuous success in staying within estimated costs. Investment cost can be highly variable, especially if a project is not completed on time. The major costs of systems development are personnel expenses; for most systems, the cost of computer time for testing and debugging is small compared to the labor cost. Our philosophy of having users design systems also makes it difficult to estimate costs in advance. The systems analyst has to estimate the number of days and average costs for computer department employees to design the system. Management may also want to allocate the salary expenses of users to the project when they are heavily involved in systems-design activities.

Once the design has progressed to the point that users know the type of response desired and have some idea of files and programs, the analyst can estimate programming requirements and costs. The best guide for these estimates is the experience of the organization on similar projects.

In contrast to development costs, operations costs are usually more predictable, at least by the time program testing has begun. These costs include charges for computer time, supplies, and labor. Sometimes all the various components of computer cost are combined into one hourly charge keyed to computer resource utilization, for example, X dollars per CPU minute, Y dollars per 1,000 lines printed, and so on. Other charging formulas are based on the units of work processed by the department, such as the number of checks processed, bills printed, and so forth.

Charge-Out Mechanisms

There have been two polar approaches to accounting for computer expenses: charging to overhead and full charge-out to users. Table 16-1 describes the advantages of each approach.

In the first approach all expenses for computers are treated as company overhead. Accounting is cheaper; it is not necessary to keep track of many individual charges or to go to the expense of developing and executing a charge-out procedure. Some advocates of this approach argue that it leaves decision making in the computer department where the technical competence to make these decisions exists. However, we have suggested that decisions should be made jointly with users.

Because of the large expenditure charged against overhead for computer expenses, it is possible that top management will review computer expenses more thoroughly under this charging system.

TABLE 16–1 **Comparison of Charging Mechanisms for Overhead Versus Full Charge-Out**

Overhead Advantages
  Cheaper
  Responsibility for control remains with computer department
  Makes all computer costs visible
  Computer expenses reviewed by top management
  Creates stability for computer department
Full Charge-Out Advantages
  Users have to allocate resources to computer services and consider
    tradeoffs for other uses of funds
  Shows how computer department is interacting with user departments
  Provides data for comparison of external services with internal
    computer service
  Provides information on relative costs of applications
  User does not see computer as a free benefit

SOURCE: From *Information Systems Concepts for Management,* 2 ed., by Henry C. Lucas, Jr. Copyright © 1982, 1978 by McGraw–Hill, Inc. Used [as edited] with the permission of McGraw–Hill Book Co.

However, there are other mechanisms to gain the attention of top management, such as budgets, plans, and steering committees. Overhead charging does create stability for the computer department since it can count on the same processing load. Conversely, under a full charge-out scheme, if user departments change their processing activities, there can be wide fluctuations in the computer department budget.

In a full charge-out scheme all computer expenses are charged to users. Users have to make resource allocation decisions; this approach leads to the complete decentralization of computer decisions. By examining the accounting system and comparing charges, management can see where the computer department is providing the most service and where it has developed the most applications. The charges make it possible to compare an internal department with an outside computer service organization, which is always an alternative to internal processing. Charging also provides data on the relative cost of each application; since the computer is not a free benefit, users may exercise more restraint in requesting systems.

The partial charge-out approach offers a flexible alternative to overhead or full charge-out accounting; the exact nature of the partial charge-out scheme depends on the individual organization. One useful approach is to charge users for operations, since a more certain amount is involved. New applications are treated as a research and development effort and are charged to overhead. This partial charge-out approach recognizes that a new computer application is a capital investment, just as is the addition of a new piece of machinery.

Some Thoughts

If You Already Charge

One of the major problems management has with computing is its steadily increasing costs. If a charging scheme exists, managers may see dramatically rising costs without any output as money is invested in the development of new applications. The applications may take a year or two to develop before there is a tangible result, but management receives the bill now.

Such a condition is particularly frustrating when the user has no real way to control the expenditures. If users are charged for services, then they should have some way to influence their charges. This means that the managers paying the bills must be involved in decisions about what systems are developed, the need to acquire new equipment to improve response times for their systems, and so on. Also, to be realistic as a rationing device, the budget for computing must not be "funny money" or funds that are not really scarce or controlled as often occurs in the university environment. When the allocated computer budget is exceeded, all I do is ask for more; such a budget is not terribly meaningful.

Finally, if you charge for services, keep it simple. A complex charging formula makes it difficult for the user to understand the bill. For example, one way to charge is so much per 1,000 lines of a report printed, so much per 100 transactions processed on a given system, so much per 1,000 characters stored on a disk, and so on.

It is simply not worth the time or cost to develop extremely sophisticated charging formulas which the typical manager cannot understand or influence.

If You Do Not Charge

A number of organizations do not charge-out computing for the reasons discussed earlier in this chapter. However, a corporate philosophy not to charge in general does not preclude charging under special circumstances. For example, one could charge when offering a new service in order to allocate its usage. We might install a package to let users develop their own reports. After a time during which the package is available free to encourage its use, it might be necessary to institute a charge for each report in order to encourage thoughtful usage of this tool.

The most important consideration in determining how to treat computing charges in any firm is the type of behavior one is trying to encourage and the state of the organization. If users are accustomed to paying for service, then a rational scheme can help control usage. If management needs to encourage the use of the system, then overhead charging is the best way to go.

CHAPTER 17

Are We Out of Control?

MANAGERS KNOW HOW TO CONTROL firms by using budgets, performance measures, quality control indicators, and similar devices. However, we seem to be reluctant to apply the same techniques to information systems. Usually there is a budget at least for the current year. However, most senior managers do not feel comfortable with it; they have little understanding of what is in the budget or of why it seems to increase steadily (even exponentially) each year.

With information systems, there are several levels of control that management needs to consider. At the lowest level, there are operating controls. The pertinent question here is whether the systems of the firm are designed and executed in such a way that the basic operations of the firm are well protected. At a higher level, control implies the ability to monitor progress and influence actions; here managers can play an important role, too. Obtaining control of information processing will help us develop confidence in this technology and learn to apply it in more creative ways.

Operational Control

I have audited computer operations on several occasions, and in at least two instances management has been extremely lucky. In these installations I would judge that information processing was out of control. The operation of the firm lacked documentation; this was the result of no planning. A major system was five years late, and all knowledge about the operation was in the head of a key individual. The operations of the firm were continuing, and management was in a blissful state of ignorance regarding just how dangerous the situation had become.

Documentation

What was wrong? First, the computer department lacked standards and documentation for programs. A program is the set of instructions that direct the computer hardware to perform operations. A program is usually written in a language that is relatively easy for the programmer to understand but very difficult, if not impossible, for the layman to read and comprehend. Even if the programmer understands a program from the standpoint of each statement in it, one may have difficulty grasping exactly what the program does. If we are talking about a system with hundreds of program modules, it can be extremely difficult to unravel the logic of the system. Finally, the task becomes more complicated when the programmer trying to understand the system is not the programmer who coded it in the first place, a frequent occurrence after a system has been operating for a while.

How are we vulnerable under such circumstances? If there is a need to perform maintenance on the program, there is no documentation to describe it. Documentation is the information that presents a road map to the program. It tells the programmer various things about the system, the purpose of various modules, how the system is constructed, and so forth. Without documentation, the programmer has to read lines of code to figure out what a program is doing—the most difficult possible way to work with a program.

Operating Controls

There is also a series of controls which should be a part of the execution of a system. For example, we have discussed various kinds of editing and totaling of figures to be certain that reports and data balance. The purpose of these controls is to insure the integrity and accuracy of the data processed or stored with each computer application. In an on-line system, we may find 60 percent or more of the code dedicated to error detection and correction.

A Key Individual

Finally, I have seen computer departments that were dependent upon one key person for their operation. This individual, due to the lack of documentation and adequate personnel, was the only person in the installation who understood how to operate applications. In one instance, this individual was responsible for all of the systems software that controlled the computer and all applications programs that performed specific tasks like inventory updating and payroll. This person could choose to leave the firm at any time, an action which would result in chaos in the computing facility and throughout the company's operations. Alternatively, the individual had tremendous opportunities to defraud the firm or sabotage operations.

What can management do to prevent these operational problems? One's accounting firm should conduct an audit of the computer department as a part of each annual certified audit; the result of this audit should be a report to management on the control of operations. You should act on this report to be sure that the operation of information systems is under control.

Service Levels

We should also be interested in the effectiveness of computer operations. In past chapters we suggested the development of user-oriented measures of service quality. I recommend that such a measure be implemented and administered at least annually, if not more often, in order to obtain a reading on how users evaluate the quality of the processing service they are receiving. Again, consider tying a part of the reward structure to the score on this evaluation. Such a control places the emphasis of operations on service, not just on running computers.

Project Control

The next level of control is at the design and operation of systems. It is very difficult for management to realize how projects are progressing unless they are involved; this means that the manager must attend review meetings and talk with subordinates about the system. How well is the system understood? What do potential users think about the chances for successful implementation?

Next, management should be sure that some type of formal management control system is being used. There are a number of commercial products available, some of which have been tailored to the management of computer projects. These packages are generally based on the critical path method. A project is broken down into various tasks with estimated completion times. The project manager sees that the system is updated and watches to see that activities on the critical path, the path that is the longest through the network of tasks, stays on schedule. The project manager may break critical tasks into several pieces to be done in parallel, assign extra resources, or decide to let the project slip.

Many computer projects are not well managed. Sometimes a critical path chart is prepared at the outset, but then efforts are not devoted to updating it over time. The project manager is dependent upon realistic input from those working on the project, many of whom do not like to have to provide data on their progress. However, by breaking tasks down into small enough components, we can ask for the completion of a task rather than an estimate of what percentage of the assignment is complete.

Project control also extends beyond whether or not systems are completed on time and within budget. Do they meet their original objectives? What are user reactions to the project? Because the development of a system is often a research and development effort, there may be legitimate reasons for cost and time to slip. Management must evaluate the reasons for problems and act accordingly; if the problem is the uncertainty of the project, they may decide to let the project slip or to assign extra resources. If the problems are due to managerial competence, then the needed action may be to improve the staff working on the project, to bring in consulting help, and so forth.

The Annual Budget

We have now established control over two important components of the function of a systems department, operations and the design of individual systems. The annual budget for these two activities is the next level of control. Does information processing stay within the guidelines of the budget? What is happening on a monthly basis? The most likely place for problems to arise is in systems design, where we may have underestimated the requirements to get a system up and running.

Charging is also a part of the budget process if we do not absorb computing in overhead. Charging is often used to control computing from the standpoint of supply and demand; users are expected to ration their use of the computing facility based on the cost to them. However, this does not always happen. At this point, it is not possible to recommend that every organization charge for information-processing services.

The Long-Term Plan

The last part of control is to see how the information services department is progressing toward achieving the goals in the three-to five-year plan. If the objective is to move more processing to end users, are we on target? If there is a program to develop more on-line systems, have the various completion dates for achieving this goal been attained? If we understand what has been accomplished and what remains to be done, then management should be able to forecast accurately the future requirements for information processing.

Summary

The message in this chapter is the key for management to gain confidence in information processing. The suggestions made here are intended to help you feel that you are in control of information processing. The approach requires that the firm has a budget, a long range plan, and ways to measure progress. It also may require some extra work on the part of accountants or a consultant to evaluate certain aspects of the operational control system.

The approach also requires active participation and input from management. If you want control, then it will be necessary to become involved in systems development projects so that you understand what is being designed; effort must be put into the planning process, reviews of progress, and budgeting for information processing. It means that the manager will have to evaluate the performance of the computing effort, both for operations and for the sum of all individual development projects. I firmly believe that this effort will pay off handsomely, both in the actual results of better control for the organization and in the feelings of confidence that it will engender. Management can and should control information processing.

A Review of the Manager's Role

The role of management is crucial to a successful information-processing effort; Table 17–1 summarizes key management activities and the reasons for them.

TABLE 17-1 Management Actions

Area	Action	Reason
Planning	See that a plan for system is developed	Foundation for system activities
Selection of Alternatives	Establish procedures	Consistency
	Insist on alternatives	Range of choices
User Design	Encourage user role	Better systems
Understanding	Learn functions	Leadership role
Policy Objectives	Promulgate management objectives, policy	Avoid system as apparent cause of change
Resource Allocation	Provide resources	Free user to participate
Reward Structure	Reward user	Motivation
Impact of System	Plan and prepare	Smooth implementation
Project Management	Monitor, use system	Maintain schedule, add resources
Evaluation of Systems Effort	Compare performance with plan	Control

The role of management begins with the planning process; a three- to five-year information-systems plan forms the foundation for guiding the systems effort and controlling it. Next, management should establish a procedure for the selection of alternatives for a new system. Few systems are infeasible; rather, the critical question is: what type of system should be developed given our present backlog and needs? Managers should also take part in the identification of critical applications areas, which should be reflected in the plan.

Managers are the people who can make user design really happen. They need the input of users; and through users designing their own systems, management will help develop more committed, better-trained users. Moreover, there are not enough analysts to do the work; users must take over some of the burden of development if they are to have computer applications.

Managers must also endeavor to understand a system and how it will function. Managers here act as leaders, encouraging users to participate actively. To do this, it may be necessary to provide extra resources; perhaps additional personnel must be hired to free existing users to work on the development of a new system. Managers may want to modify the reward structure, to pay bonuses partially based on the success of a system or on an individual's making a major contribution to it.

Management must see that the organization understands the implications of a system. Will users be prepared for the impact of the system? Have we considered everything possible to be sure that there is a smooth installation? Managers must also monitor the development of a system to see that the project remains in control.

Finally, management must evaluate the performance of the entire information-processing effort. Compare the performance of the system's function with the original plan. This high-level examination of the plan is the first step in achieving management control of information processing.

Douglas McGregor, a noted labor relations expert, once said that, by and large, companies get the kind of labor relations they deserve. I think this statement applies equally well to systems: management gets the kind of information processing it deserves!

CHAPTER 18

How Does a Computer Really Work?

ONE OF THE MAJOR PROBLEMS managers have in dealing with computers is the foreign nature of the technology. We have invented a new language and terms that are quite different from ordinary experience. In this chapter, I shall try to unravel some of the mysteries of computers and their functions. However, in order to keep the discussion manageable and somewhat readable, it will be necessary to simplify what is a complex and elegant technology. We shall deal with the technology at a conceptual level and shall try to answer some of the questions which I have found bother managers.

Introduction

The first thing we must do is to distinguish between hardware and software. Hardware is easy to define—it is what you can see and feel. You can walk up to a piece of hardware and kick it! Software, on the other hand, is a set of instructions which tells the computer what to do. I hope that the nature of software will become a little more clear as we progress through the chapter.

I shall, in the next section, discuss how a general computer operates. Then we shall cover each generation of computer in turn to see how the technology has changed and to obtain a feeling for how software has developed. At the end, the objective is for the reader to be more comfortable with computing technology.

Figure 18–1 is a simple block diagram of a computer. There are two components whose operations we need to understand first. Begin with primary memory which is able to store information. At the lowest level, the memory is capable of holding a series of 0's and 1's or bits. Physically, memory consists of devices that have two states; for example, we could represent a 1 as the presence of a voltage on a transistor and a 0 as the lack of a voltage. Since it is difficult for people to work with 0 and 1, memory is usually organized into groups of 0's and 1's which form characters. A character is like a letter, a, b, c, or any other keyboard symbol. Each character may be treated alone, or groups of characters may be formed as "words." On some machines, eight of the bits described above form a character, and four characters form a word.

We must also have ways of putting information into memory and retrieving it. For these reasons, each block of storage has an address, sometimes at the character level and sometimes at the word level. Assume for argument's sake that we can address each word in memory. The address is like the number on your mailbox; it tells where your house is located on a street. We know nothing

FIGURE 18–1   A Simple Computer

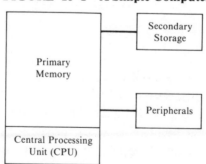

about the contents of the mailbox until we open it and look inside. In the computer, the address says where something is located in memory, not what is there.

Memory is passive, it only holds data. The power of the computer is in the central processing unit or CPU; this device controls all of the operations of the computer. The CPU can store and retrieve data from memory. The CPU also has registers that perform arithmetic operations on data. Remember that at the lowest level we are dealing with a series of 1's and 0's which form the binary system. Engineers have devised electronic devices which can add, subtract, multiply, and divide these numbers. The central processing unit then executes instructions that command it to retrieve data from memory, add it to other data, move it back into memory, and so on; the instructions are more or less wired into the computer. When the CPU sees a certain configuration of characters in an instruction, it is wired to execute that instruction, be it an add, subtract, or any of the other instructions the machine is programmed to understand.

Man is one of the most flexible "computers" around; most people with an elementary education are able to execute clear instructions. Consider the following set of instructions:

Ask the person next to you for a number.

Write it on line 1.

Ask the person next to you for another number.

Write it on line 2.

Add the numbers on lines 1 and 2.

Write the answer on line 3.

Tell the person next to you the answer from line 3.

This is a simple set of instructions to a human computer. You know how, that is, you are "wired" to execute each instruction. You know how to ask for a number, how to write, add, and tell the answer.

The series of instructions written above constitutes a program, in this case a program to take two numbers and to add them together. In a computer, a program is a set of instructions which can be interpreted by the computer. When the computer gets to each instruction, it executes it. The addition instruction is wired into the computer, just as you know how to add numbers from long years of learning and practice.

The analogy with a human breaks down soon, however. In the human program, we used voice communications; you asked someone for numbers and spoke the answer. There are computers that can play answers back from prerecorded syllables, and there is even some progress on speech input; but for the most part, computers communicate with the outside world through peripheral devices. A typical input device is a terminal with a human typing data into the computer. In the early days, a great deal of input was done with the familiar punched card. Output peripherals include the line printer, the terminal used as an output device, and similar components.

The last block on the figure is something called secondary storage. This kind of storage differs from primary memory. It is usually much larger and less expensive; it stores large amounts of data that are not needed on-line all of the time. The most common secondary storage devices are magnetic tapes and disks. (In the next chapter we shall discuss these devices more fully.)

The critical difference with primary memory is the way we access the data on secondary storage. In primary memory, the central processing unit can access any location in a very short period of time, say 50 nanoseconds (50 *billionths* of a second). For data in secondary storage, the computer must access the storage device and move the data to primary memory. For a disk this may take an average of 30 milliseconds (30 thousandths of a second), roughly a million times longer than it does when working with data that are already in primary memory.

The First Generation

We have discussed simple computers without much detail. Their operations are probably not very clear, but perhaps tracing their development will make today's computers a little easier to understand. See Table 18-1.

In the first generation, computers were constructed of vacuum tubes. They were large, tended to fail often, and took large amounts of electricity to run.

From a software standpoint, the first computers were programmed in machine language, the sequence of numbers that the machine could understand. Programmers found it hard to work with these numbers and so developed a computer language with which it would be easier for humans to work. They invented a computer language which included instructions like

GET Y

ADD X

STO Z

to get data located at some position Y, then add data from X, and store the results at location Z. Instead of programmers having to tell the computer in numbers what instruction to execute and what location to use for the numbers X, Y, and Z, the computer could do this itself.

We could teach a clerk how to take a program in our language above and translate it into the string of numbers a computer actually needs to execute the program. However, the instructions to the clerk would be so clear and well-structured that we could actually program a computer to do the translation. Thus, we see a computer helping programmers use the computer more effectively! The language we have just developed with GET Y and ADD X was called assembly language, and the translation program is known as an assembler.

Still, programmers were not satisfied. An assembler might be all right for the professional programmer who coded all the time, but what about the scientist or engineer who only needed to program occasionally? It was too hard to work in assembly language and to remember all of the instructions. As an engineer, I want to say $Z = X + Y$ and let the computer do the rest. My statement is in a higher-level language, that is, the language does more things in each statement than does assembly language. A group of users

TABLE 18-1 Computer Generations

GENERATION	YEAR	HARDWARE	SOFTWARE	INNOVATIONS	EXAMPLES
1	1950s	Vacuum tube	Machine language	Assembly language FORTRAN Operating system	IBM 650, 709
2	1960s	Transistors	Assembler Higher-level languages Operating system	Time-sharing On-line system	IBM 1401, 7090
3	1965	Integrated circuits	Operating system Higher-level language	Microprogramming Multiprogramming Time-sharing Virtual memory	IBM 360 line
3½	1971	Semiconductor primary memory	Virtual memory Telecommunications Data-base management	Packages	IBM 370
4	1980s	Large-scale integration	More packages Program generators	Coming	IBM 4300, 3081

formed a committee and developed the first such higher-level language called FORTRAN for FORmula TRANslation, a language which is still widely used today. A translator for a higher-level language is called a compiler.

In this first generation, an operator ran the computer totally. He or she scheduled all of the jobs on the machine, loaded tape drives, took paper off the printer, and so on. Remember, at this time all processing was in batch, there were no on-line systems with terminal access. Jobs were taken from punch cards or tapes, loaded one by one into the computer, and executed.

A group of users decided to try to automate some of the operator's tasks by writing a simple program. The program would take charge of processing and perform some of the functions done by the operator. For example, the program would recognize that I wanted to translate a FORTRAN program and call the compiler for this task. This program is known as an operating system; it is part of something we call "systems software," programs that run the computer rather than do direct work for users.

The Second Generation

In the second half of the 1950s, the transistor was applied to the logic circuits of a computer, resulting in a tremendous increase in speed and reduction in cost. Programmers began to work with more higher-level languages. The U.S. Department of Defense pushed hard for the adoption of a high-level language for business processing called COBOL (COmmon Business Oriented Language), the most frequently used language in the U.S. today.

Though their use was not universal, operating systems began to become more popular. There were still a great many programs written in assembly language, but we saw increasingly more movement toward higher-level languages.

At MIT, researchers grew tired of waiting—sometimes days—for their jobs to be returned from a computer operating in batch mode. It occurred to them that a computer was very fast and could serve a number of slow humans working at terminals. Why not have a group of people all simultaneously share the central processing unit and other resources of the computer? The researchers developed a powerful time-sharing system based on this concept.

While user #1 is thinking about his program, the computer brings in the program of user #2 from secondary storage and executes it. While user #2 is thinking, it switches back to the program for user #1. Actually, the computer is so fast it does not have to wait for a think break from a user; it can actually serve user #2 while user #1 is typing. To each user it appears that he is working on his own, responsive computer. (While great in theory, one *does* notice a slowdown in such a system when there are numerous users; in the case of the first system, this slowdown became so pronounced at 32 users that no further users were allowed on the system.)

Simultaneously, industry was taking note of the military command and control systems that allowed decision makers to interact with computers on-line. The most immediate need was for airline reservations. A clerk located any place in the U.S. needed up-to-the-second knowledge of the status of flights. Old systems also did not associate a name with a reservation, which led to a lot of errors. American Airlines in conjunction with IBM developed the SABRE airline reservations system, the first on-line, passenger-name reservations system. Today, almost every major airline has such a system or shares one with another carrier.

The Third Generation

The third generation is characterized by the development of integrated circuits in which a number of electrical components are fabricated on a single chip of semiconducting material. This process is known as Large Scale Integration (LSI). The third generation created many problems for the manufacturers of computers and eventually for users. During the first generation relatively few programs had been developed, so converting to the second generation was not too painful. Why, you may ask, couldn't you simply run the programs from the first generation on the computers of the second?

It would have been nice if things worked out that way. Unfortunately, every designer developed something a little differently when building a computer. As a result, at the machine-language level there is virtually no compatibility among computers. My first-generation computer programs are entirely different from those for the second generation, at least at the assembly and machine-language level. One of the motivations for higher-level languages was to make it easier to use programs interchangeably among different computers.

For the third generation, IBM in particular wanted to develop a family of computers so that programs from one could be executed on another; this necessitated having a series of instructions common to all the computers in that family. Until this time, one received more instructions and more powerful instructions with larger, more expensive computers. IBM was also faced with a conversion problem; how could it now sell computers to clients and obsolete all of their second-generation programs? No one would quietly accept writing off that investment.

The answer to these problems opened a whole new set of opportunities for the industry. The third generation of computers introduced something known as microprogramming—"firmware," since it is partway between hardware and software.

Each instruction in a computer can really be broken down into a much smaller series of "micro" instructions. Visualize a large instruction made of a set of smaller building blocks; some of these building blocks will be common to all of the larger instructions. Thus, we can build an instruction from a series of smaller instructions.

It is actually cheaper to build a complex instruction this way than to "wire it into" the computer; therefore, we can use microprogramming extensively to create instructions that look like the wired-in instructions on the top of the line computer. Thus we can have instruction sets with universal components in our series of computers.

How did this help solve the marketing problems of converting second generation programs to third? We could use a combination of software programs and these microprogrammed instructions to make the third generation computer simulate the second generation it replaced. Thus we could replace the second generation and take our time to write new programs for the third-generation machine. In addition, because the third generation was so much faster than the second, we could actually run simulated programs faster on the third-generation computer than they had run on the second! This simulation process became known generally as emulation, the use of hardware and software to make one computer act like another. Today microprogramming and firmware are used extensively because they are faster than software and more adaptable than hardwiring.

Now we could launch the third generation, using integrated circuits. For the first time, the operating system was an integral part of the computer; we could not really run one without it. The simple program had evolved into a complex piece of systems software which supported the operator and provided many functions for the programmer as well. Almost all programming after this time would be done in higher-level languages.

We also found that the central processing unit in the second generation of computers was not very busy; the peripheral and secondary storage devices took the time and the CPU was often idle, perhaps 60 percent or more of the day. To make this relatively expensive component more productive during the third generation, we applied time-sharing concepts to batch processing. By writing and utilizing a sophisticated operating system, it was possible to hold multiple programs in a semi-active state in primary storage simultaneously. When one program was blocked to do input or output, for example, the central processing unit would be assigned by the operating system to work on another program. This concept, known as multiprogramming, increased the number of programs that could get through the computer in a given period of time. It also became possible, through the operating system, to attach more than one central processor to systems—a strategy called "multiprocessing"—when the processor needed help, such as in performing scientific calculations.

Conditions were not static on the time-sharing front, either. The MIT group found that programmers working with time-sharing quickly ran out of primary memory. The research group developed a system which provided the appearance of an almost limitless memory; the operating system kept all of a user's program in secondary storage and brought pieces of it into primary memory when needed for execution. These pieces or pages were never all in primary memory at one time. The term given to this almost infinite memory was "virtual memory."

Three and One-half Generations

In the late 60s and early 70s, third-generation computers evolved further. While not as dramatic as in past generations, major improvements in technology and some improvements in software occurred. In relation to hardware, the core memory—ferrite cores that were magnetized in different directions to represent 1's and 0's—gave way to semiconductor memory. Semiconductors were much faster and contributed greatly to an increase in computer speed.

Regarding software, the increase in demand for on-line systems was supported by vendors with systems software created to manage large amounts of data, to facilitate communications across long distances, and to develop applications. Virtual memory was applied to batch systems as well as to time-sharing. Parts of the operating system were written in firmware to enhance their execution.

The Fourth Generation

New technology featuring greater circuit integration, that is, more components on a chip and increased speed of function, characterizes fourth-generation technology. Change in the fourth generation has been highly evolutionary. The hardware has remained similar to that of the third generation; newer computers are faster and feature larger memory. However, the program-conversion process is simpler because the fourth-generation hardware closely resembles that of the third in terms of machine language.

The proliferation of packages and software is significant. New programs generate code for the programmer in a short period of time; these generators are like enhanced higher-level languages. Also, we find more user-oriented systems that allow the end user himself to program simple retrieval requests.

Today's Confusion

Today we are in the beginning stages of the fourth generation. The changes of our time, however, are more evolutionary than revolutionary because of the huge investment that already exists in software. The evolution will continue, with much emphasis shifting to the further development of software.

We ignored one complication in the above analysis; the development of the minicomputer and then of the microcomputer. We have explored the characteristics of the various generations of computers by focusing primarily on what are called "mainframe" computers. At first, these were the only machines available. However, during the third generation, advances in the fabrication (Large Scale Integration) of circuit components drastically reduced the cost of logic and memory. (Very Large Scale Integration [VSLI] is expected to reduce that even further; millions or even billions of components are expected to be placed on wafers the size of postage stamps in the coming years.)

Initially, small components were used to develop minicomputers, machines that typically had short word lengths and a simple, dedicated operating system (e.g., for time-sharing). At first, minicomputers were applied to a single task. Minicomputers have been used in process control applications and as the basis for "intelligent terminals," that is, terminals with their own logic such as programs for editing local data. One dynamic graphics CRT terminal—a terminal capable of drawing figures—is a TV set controlled by a minicomputer. Minis have even been used aboard yachts to compute variables during a race. Many businesses have purchased minicomputers to use their time-sharing operating systems to develop relatively inexpensive on-line systems.

Applications have expanded in two directions from the first minicomputers. The development of even less expensive fabrication techniques and logic made it possible to expand the size and capabilities of the mini and to create the "supermini." At the other extreme, we have seen the development of computers on a chip. These tiny microcomputers promise to revolutionize industry. A microcomputer usually has smaller word size and is slower than a mini; however, a micro is frequently used in dedicated applications where extremely high speeds are not required. Micros have been employed in standard information-processing tasks and in a variety of industrial products. For example, many automobiles use microprocessors to control fuel/air mixtures by taking into account parameters like the load on the engine, pollution output of the car, and temperature. Microprocessors are appearing in more and more products because they offer sophisticated logic at very low cost.

Table 18–2 describes the major characteristics that can be used to distinguish among types of computers from large mainframes to smaller micros. Of course, the categories really represent points on a continuum; there is a great deal of overlap even within the line of a single manufacturer.

Because of the availability of mini- and microcomputers, we have been treated to a new trend in the field, distributed processing. We discussed this concept under types of organizations in Chapter 7. The idea is that end users can have control over a computer system, hardware, software, and all aspects of systems development and management. There are significant management implications for these choices which we tried to explain earlier.

Low-priced technology makes all of this possible. According to IBM, 25 years ago it cost $1.26 to do 100,000 multiplications, while today it costs less than one-half cent. From another perspec-

TABLE 18–2 Types of Computer Systems

TYPE	SPEED MIPS*	COST (000)	MAIN MEMORY K bytes	SECONDARY STORAGE bytes	SOFTWARE	APPLICATIONS
Mainframes	.5–10	300	500	5×10^8 to 10×10^9	Extensive operating systems, applications packages	Batch, time-sharing, on-line transactions processing simultaneously
Superminis	.1–2	150–500	256+ Virtual	10^8 to 10^9	Time-sharing Limited batch	Specialized, scientific, engineering, transactions processing
Minis	.1–.5	30–150	16–256	10^6 to 10^8	Time-sharing	General-purpose time-sharing, small commercial applications on-line
Micros	.001–.5	Under 10	8–256	5×10^6	Simple operating system	Dedicated applications, limited I/O, e.g., intelligent terminals, word processors, small business systems

*MIPS = millions of instructions per second

SOURCE: From *Information Systems Concepts for Management*, 2 ed., by Henry C. Lucas, Jr. Copyright © 1982, 1978 by McGraw–Hill, Inc. Used [as edited] with the permission of McGraw–Hill Book Co.

tive, we see large computers which can already execute 100 million instructions per second—and the ultimate capacity has not yet been established!

In conclusion, the most significant point for the manager is that hardware is constantly becoming more powerful and less expensive. In fact, since the first days of computers this trend has been true. Why then, may you ask, are my firm's computing costs increasing every year? There are two answers to this question. First, the amount of computing you are doing is undoubtedly greater now than it was in the past. Second, the cost of developing applications is labor intensive, and the skilled labor needed is becoming more scarce and more expensive.

Due to declining hardware costs, we must use computer hardware more inefficiently in order to reduce the high applications backlog that exists in firms today. I think that users grasp at distributed processing because they can set priorities and perhaps have an application developed before five years have elapsed. They do not see the problems of coordination or of managing a data center. Instead, they see the hope of cheap technology letting them develop an application they need.

How can we use computers less efficiently, substitute mass-produced technology for difficult-to-find human labor? We shall run package programs that do not use a computer efficiently but can be implemented quickly. We shall give end users the ability to write requests in simple retrieval languages which take more computer power to execute. In every way possible, we will begin to treat the systems designer, rather than the hardware, as the scarce resource.

CHAPTER 19

What Are Files and Data Bases?

IN THE PREVIOUS CHAPTER we talked about secondary storage devices which store large amounts of data, billions of characters. We cannot fit all of these data into primary memory at one time, and it would be wasteful to have them there, anyway. Little of the data is accessed frequently, but it all needs to be available at some point in time. In this chapter we describe data storage in a little more detail. Files are of extreme importance; they determine what type of processing we can do in a system.

Fundamentals

Before discussing the use of storage, we need to focus on the way in which data are stored in a computer. In the last chapter we mentioned that we are usually interested in characters. In a file, we group characters to form a field; as an example, consider the characters in your last name. We might allow 15 characters in a field for the last name. We begin a last name in the leftmost character; any spaces remaining at the end are blank.

Generally we are interested in a set of information about someone, certainly more than a last name. Therefore we group fields of data together to form something called a record. In the example above, we might have fields for last names, first name, age, social security number, rate of pay, deductions, and so on. It is easy to envision our record consisting of 20 or more fields and a total of several hundred characters.

If this is a payroll or personnel system, we would have one of these records for every person in the firm. To identify the individual, we would probably use a payroll number that we assigned or possibly the social security number.

Why do we use numbers instead of names? We seem to be deluged with numbers. A computer can be programmed to use names to identify records; the trouble is that such a procedure is more difficult for the computer (no real excuse for not doing it) and is also more prone toward error. People are not consistent in the ways they write and spell their names; sometimes they sign with full first names, other times they give initials only. In addition, a large firm potentially has two or more people with identical names, so the use of a number has quite a few advantages.

Sequential Files

Sequential files consist of records maintained in some order, such as by payroll number. This means that the record of the person with the lowest employee number would be the first one on the file. Subsequent records would be located in a linear sequence on a magnetic tape or disk until we reached the record of the employee with the highest payroll number.

Why bother with keeping the tape in order? A file of data has to be constantly updated in most applications. Suppose that we are changing the rate of pay for 100 employees this month. The computer must have a way to alter the pay rate field for just those 100 employees and not others. Because the file is in sequence, we will process one record at a time. Remember that the total amount of data on the file is likely to be too much to fit in primary memory at one time, so we read a record at a time from the tape by putting it into primary memory. If the 100 employees to be changed are on another tape in random order and the master file of records for the payroll is also in random order, we will spend a long time changing the pay rates.

We would read one change, say for employee # 500. We then must read the master file until we find employee # 500. After making this change, we must then read another change, say for employee # 300. Now we must back up on the master file and find the record for employee # 300; this is a rather clumsy procedure.

However, if we keep the master file in sequence and then sort the change file into the same sequence, we can match the two against each other without backing up. We read employee # 300 first and move to his or her record in the master file. Finishing with that change, we read a change for employee # 500. Now move the master file forward to employee # 500, and so on. This is a relatively efficient way to update this tape by processing it once and making all changes. As mentioned in an earlier chapter, this is how we developed the name batch processing; transactions (changes in this case) are batched together and run at one time to update the tape file.

There is one last complication, but it actually facilitates updating of the tape. The physical tape drive does not allow one to read and write on the same tape; also, we would not want to do so from a control standpoint. If our program had an error in it, we could write over some important information on the master file. In addition, we keep all of the records contiguous on the tape although it is quite possible that a new employee might join the firm and be assigned a payroll number that is between two existing numbers, say # 450. We would not want to anticipate this addition by leaving a blank record on the master file—who knows how many there might be?

As a result of all of these problems, when we update a sequential file, the file is actually recreated. That is, we process the transactions against the old master file and write a new copy of the master file with the changes on a separate tape drive. As a bonus, we have automatic backup. If we keep the old master file and the transactions, we can easily recreate the new file if something happens to it.

Suppose that, as a manager, you want to make some changes to this system. Assume that you want to add information about where every employee works in the firm in the form of a department number. It should be easy, but often it may turn out to take a long time and a lot of money. What is happening? If your changes require adding new data to an existing file, the size of the records will have to be changed to accommodate the new information. Since the data must come from someplace, it will have to be added to some input form that is now in use or a new one will have to be developed. Remember that we edit input data, so a program will have to be modified to edit for legitimate department numbers. Every program that uses the file contains a definition of the record, and each of these will have to be modified to reflect either the new information in the record or at least its increase in size. Finally, program instructions will have to be written to actually update the file with the department number. And this was a simple change!

Important principle: *It is far easier to make changes during the design stage than it is after a system has been programmed.*

You have probably heard about retrieval programs that allow you to develop your own reports. These packages are very powerful as long as the information wanted is already in a file or set of files. With some training, a user can learn how to write programs that do quite elegant retrievals. Of course, there will have to be support from the computer staff who know the format of the records and where the files are located. An example of such a retrieval might provide a report of all employees who have more than five dependents and a salary of over $10,000 per year. Because the retrieval program must go through the entire sequential file, we generally batch retrieval requests and process them at one point in time, possibly just after updating the master file. While you can get the answer to your question, it will certainly not be instantaneous; you may wait several hours or even days for the results.

Direct Access

If you really want immediate access to data, like the airline reservations agent who must know the status of flight reservations up to the moment, then a type of file other than the sequential file must be used. The direct-access file, usually stored on some kind of computer disk device, is the answer; it is used in virtually all on-line systems.

Physically, a disk looks like a series of long-playing phonograph records stacked on top of each other with some space between them. The disk rotates at a high rate of speed. In the spaces between layers there are read/write heads which can access data that have been stored on each platter. The platters are actually coated with magnetic material so that the recording is quite similar to what is on a tape; only now the physical characteristics of the device make it possible to reach any point on the surface at random. If you recall from our discussion of hardware, however, it takes a long time to do this—on the order of thousandths of a second while the computer is operating at speeds of 50 billionths of a second.

As you would expect, the disk is more expensive than a tape. Therefore, we still find many applications using tape; and in fact, we use tape to make a back-up copy of what is on the disk in order to recover from a system failure. Still, there are many organizations that literally have billions of characters of data on-line at one time.

This sounds easy, but there must be something more than meets the eye. Yes, we can locate information at any place on the disk, but the problem is that we have to know where the information is located. Suppose that we have a file which contains orders for a product that we sell. The file is organized by order number. For historical reasons, we have a 7-digit order number because two of the digits indicate which warehouse stocks the item. If we have a question about order number 1234567, where do we find its record on the disk?

Obviously, we could search the disk and look for it; but if this is our strategy, we might as well have used a tape because we are treating the disk like a sequential file. It is up to the analyst and programmer to devise a way of mapping the number 1234567 into an address on the disk where the record is stored. One simple way to do this is shown in Figure 19–1. We have a large possible set of keys, not all of which will be used, and we want to transform them into an address of a record on the disk.

One way to do this is to have something called a dictionary, a type of directory, in the primary memory of the computer. The dictionary contains only two pieces of data for each disk record, the key and the address of the record on the disk. If our order number is at disk address 300, the dictionary entry would be 1234567, 300. Now the program reads the key entered, searches its dictionary in high speed primary memory to find the address 300, and retrieves record 300 from the disk where the data about this order have been stored.

That was nice; we have virtually instantaneous retrieval. Why not ask a more complicated question now? Tell me all of the orders which must be shipped by the 31st of this month. Again, the naive strategy is to search each record and look at each date for shipment field. Such brute force would work, but can be rather time-consuming if there are 100,000 records in the file and only 10 percent are likely to have a shipping date of the 31st.

As an alternative, we can build a directory on shipping date. The directory would show each possible shipping date and point to the first occurrence of that date in the file (See Figure 19–2).

FIGURE 19–1 Record Location on the Disk

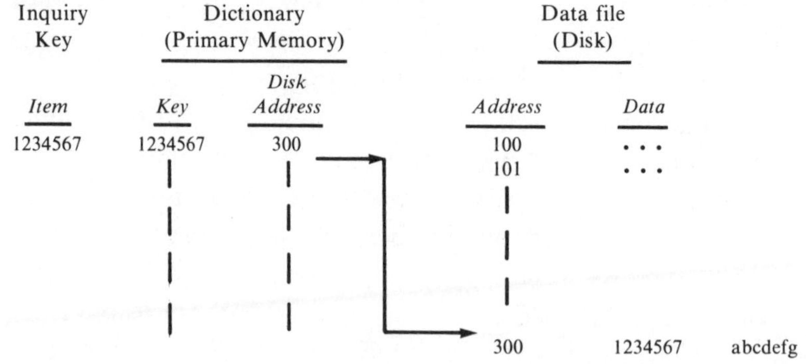

Inquiry Key	Dictionary (Primary Memory)		Data file (Disk)	
Item	*Key*	*Disk Address*	*Address*	*Data*
1234567	1234567	300	100	. . .
			101	. . .
			300	1234567 abcdefg

Directory
(Primary Memory)

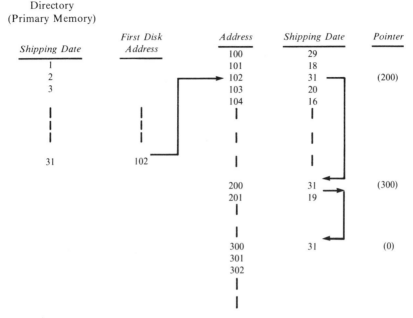

FIGURE 19-2 **Search on Shipping Date**

The next trick is to locate the second record with a shipping date of the 31st. One way is to have something called a pointer that points from the first order for the 31st to the next order with the same shipping date. We could do this by having the pointer right in the file or by having a list of record addresses in the directory for each record with the given shipping date.

Our physical data in the example above has been stored seemingly at random on the disk. However, by constructing directories and using different kinds of pointers, we have created different logical structures. For the inquiry on shipping date, it looks as if we have a chain that lists all records with a given shipping date. The directories are called indices and they describe information about how to access the file; they turn the physical data structure into a logical one that matches the users' view.

Now what about changes? Suppose that you come back after the system has been operating for a while and ask for changes. You would now like to have the ability to inquire about product number and to see all orders for a given product. The logic is quite similar to our retrieval on shipping date, but the problem is that we have not planned to retrieve on the key of product number. That means there are no directories which have been built and no inquiry programs that allow you to make such a request from a terminal. Remember that the request must be edited and checked for validity; for example, do we make something with that product number? We may have to conduct major surgery on the system to modify programs, files, and indices to accommodate your request.

It is far easier to make changes during the design stage than it is after a system has been programmed.

One of the reasons for stressing strong user involvement in the design portion of the process is to help reduce the number of expensive and time-consuming changes that will have to be made later on. Knowledgeable user input can significantly reduce the amount of redesign and reprogramming needed after the system has been installed.

Data Base

For the last decade, one of the major trends in the field has been the adoption of data-base management systems. A data-base management system (DBMS) is a set of systems software programs, a type of package program which we discuss in the next chapter. The DBMS, however, is more than a set of programs; it is a design philosophy.

In the early days of programming, each system or program owned its data. The program processed entire records at a time, and there was much duplication of data. A bank might have a separate loan system, mortgage system, and savings system. If a customer had multiple dealings with the bank, his name would appear in each system along with basic information like social security number and address.

The concept behind a data base is that we try to separate the program and the data to the greatest extent possible. Of course, one can never have total data independence, but we can move farther in that direction. The data-base system also provides an access method. Now the program does not ask for a record; instead, it requests just the fields desired (as shown in Figure 19–3) and the data-base management system accesses the data.

But how does the system know where the data are, and who manages the data base? We have created a new speciality in the organization, the data-base administrator or DBA. The DBA uses a language provided with the DBMS to describe the physical and logical relationships among data. The data description is referenced by the DBMS to determine where the fields requested by the program are located on the disk. The DBMS then is responsible for maintaining indices and putting in pointers, something done automatically by software given the description in the language.

The task of the DBA is to be sure that data are identified and well structured. For example, consider a firm in which a term like shipping date has multiple meanings depending on the country! In some places "shipping date" means the date the item is available for shipping, in others it is the date the item is on the dock waiting for the truck, and in one it is the date goods arrive at the customer location. The DBA must find a common definition and a common name; we do not want to store the same data twice or have multiple meanings for it.

FIGURE 19–3 The Data Base Management System

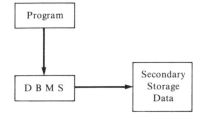

Data definition
language describes
physical and logical
views of data.

Is the organization of the future going to have one huge data base? The answer is probably no. Instead, a DBMS will be acquired to facilitate the development of one system, e.g., order entry. It will take a large initial investment to acquire the system, to learn to use it, and to begin to apply DB concepts to design. However, after gaining experience and developing an application, the DBMS will be used for new applications such as production control. The second system should be considerably easier to program than was the first, since it appears that there are significant productivity gains after the initial learning period.

Changes should be easier, too. Now only the programs actually affected by the change have to be altered. If a new field becomes a key, we do not have to change every program; we change only programs using that field, since retrieval requests for data are at the level of the field, not that of the entire record. The DBA can make many changes; programmers have to change only the programs specifically affected.

Summary

We have come a long way from the simple sequential tape file. To a great extent, the development of systems now revolves around the data and how we want to access it. The two important messages from this chapter are to design "up front," put effort into designing the system you really want before large amounts of money are invested in programming. Use techniques like a simple prototype or simulation to test parts of the design, and then develop the final system.

Second, be prepared for data-base management systems. There will be a large initial cost and a period of time needed to organize for use of the system; but once that investment has been made, there should be valuable returns in productivity and flexibility. If we use the best available technology and work together to design systems, applications can be responsive to users and to management.

CHAPTER 20

What's in a Package?

FOR MORE THAN TEN YEARS I have heard that the solution to all of our problems lies in software packages. After initial skepticism, I am becoming convinced that this is at least one of the possible approaches to diminishing the backlog of applications; in the typical firm there are many more requests for systems than there are resources to develop them.

A software package is a set of programs written by a vendor or software house for use by multiple customers. The major problem with packages is in determining what factors are associated with successful implementation. I have seen examples of highly successful packages—and equally disastrous package implementations. I am disturbed that, as yet, we have no clear understanding of preconditions for successful implementation.

In lieu of more precise guidelines, I recommend that an organization first determine what it wants to accomplish before talking to the package salesman. Define your requirements, even to the point of a high-level systems design, and then look for packages or systems that fit these needs. Without your own plan to act as a benchmark, it is too easy to be swayed by the intriguing features of a package that are not needed in your situation.

Prepare a set of your own specifications against which to judge the capabilities of any package or turnkey system.

Package Programs

The software vendor tries to develop a computer application which can be used by a number of different organizations. Since it is then unnecessary for each organization to program its own system, costs can be reduced. This idea seems appealing; what are its advantages and disadvantages? We shall examine this question from the viewpoints of the vendor and of the customer.

The vendor wants to produce a package which is very general, in order to increase market potential and to reduce the need for modifications. To accomplish this purpose, two strategies can be followed. A package which features a number of input parameters or tables can be produced; the customer provides many of these parameters only once to initial the package. Another approach is to develop a package with various modules; the client configures a package containing only the modules needed. Many times a vendor employs a combination of these two approaches.

The idea of a package system has been combined with the low cost of mini- and microcomputers. There are a number of vendors who offer complete systems on what is called a turnkey basis; the vendor contracts to supply a computer and programmer and to turn the system over to the user. As an example, a client held a series of meetings with users to develop a high-level plan for information systems in the firm. We sent the specifications to vendors for bids and evaluated the results. For the first time, the type of software packages available was more important to our evaluation than was the hardware. In fact, we took our last-choice hardware because a turnkey vendor had a good system which operated only on one manufacturer's hardware.

From the customer's viewpoint, why use a package? First, the costs of developing information systems are steadily increasing. Designing and programming a computer-based information system is a labor-intensive task. Maintenance of existing systems requires 50 to 80 percent of programming time, leaving little for developing new applications. In addition, 200 to 300 percent overruns on cost and time are not unusual when developing custom software in-house.

Packages offer one way to reduce costs and to shorten development time. In addition, many small organizations do not wish to establish their own computer departments; with a package, the design and operation of computer systems can be left to an outside firm. One large beverage manufacturer buys 20 percent of its applications software; other firms are following the same trend.

The customer, however, often does not want a package as general as the vendor's product may be; the client wants the package to do a particular job. From a user's standpoint, a collection of functions in excess of those needed can be detrimental—they result in less efficient programs and more complex input and installation efforts.

There are numerous examples of package programs. One vendor offers a batch data-management retrieval and report generator package which has been highly successful. On the basis of input requests, the program reads data from several files and extracts the requested information by using logical combinations of variables specified by the user. It is possible to perform computations on the data and to print totals and subtotals.

The user employs structured forms to describe the information to be retrieved and the format of output reports. There is a substantial use of default options, that is, standard values for an input as assured unless otherwise entered. For example, a package might automatically print the data and page number on the upper right-hand side of a report unless specifically requested otherwise. Default options reduce the input requirements for the average user.

The retrieval package outlined above provides reporting flexibility, since each individual requesting a report can custom-tailor it to his or her needs. Some information services departments have succeeded in having user departments prepare input directly; a user rather than a computer professional is responsible for the use of the system in each department.

To illustrate the diversity of packages, consider a dedicated package, that is, a package to which an entire computer system is dedicated. One computer vendor developed a special operating system and series of applications programs for an airline passenger reservations system.

The development of such a system is a very complex undertaking; the vendor tries to reduce the costs and effort involved (the vendor expended an estimated 400 person-years or more of effort in developing this package). However, the client airline still has to provide much data and will probably modify the package. It is necessary for the user to supply data that differs among airlines, such as routes and schedules.

The airline must also train agents and prepare for a massive implementation effort. Continued modification and maintenance are required after the installation of the system. By making changes and correcting errors, the vendor continually updates the system; these changes must be made in the user's version of the system.

These examples should illustrate the broad range of applications in which packages have proven successful. While there are many advantages and disadvantages of these packages, on balance we expect to see more use of packages in the future because of the high cost of developing special-purpose programs. We can afford to use computer hardware less efficiently as technology reduces the cost per computation, particularly as the cost of human resources increases.

Evaluation

Many times a package will be considered as an alternative to developing a system in-house. Before choosing a package, the information services department and a user committee should agree

TABLE 20-1   Considerations in Evaluating Software Packages

Functions included	Changes required in existing system
Modifications required to package	to use package
Installation effort	Vendor support
User interface	Updating of package
Flexibility	Documentation
Execution time	Cost and terms

SOURCE: From *Information Systems Concepts for Management,* 2 ed., by Henry C. Lucas, Jr. Copyright © 1982, 1978 by McGraw-Hill, Inc. Used [as edited] with the permission of McGraw-Hill Book Co.

on criteria for screening packages. Table 20-1 lists some of the possible evaluation criteria for decisions on applications packages. The major reason for acquiring a package is that it performs a desired function; one needs to know how many desired functions are included and what effort would be required to modify the package.

It is important to consider the user interface; that is, how difficult is it to use the package? How much information does the user have to supply? Is it simple to prepare and to understand the input? Is the package flexible? That is, can it be used if requirements change somewhat?

The evaluation is also concerned with execution time of the package and its impact on current computer operations. Execution time considerations are not important for a simple application which is run infrequently, but speed can be essential to a major dedicated system. The user needs to know the extent to which present procedures must change to accommodate the new package.

It is necessary to evaluate the software vendor's support and the likelihood that a vendor will remain in business. It does not require much in the way of resources to program and to sell software packages. Updates and improvements to the package should be forthcoming, and we are dependent on the vendor's remaining in business.

With software packages, documentation is extremely important; the information services department staff may have to modify the package and will undoubtedly have to correct errors that occur. Users are concerned with documentation as well, since documentation, combined with whatever training the vendor provides, must be sufficient to allow users to interact with the package. The final consideration is cost; we should remember that we usually both underestimate the cost of developing a comparable system ourselves and overestimate the cost of modifying a package.

Many of the criteria in Table 20-1 require the analysis of package documentation by the systems analyst and programming staff. We should also contact present users to inquire about vendor claims and support. Almost all the recommended criteria are subjective; therefore, several individuals should rank the package on each criterion, for example, on a 1 to 7 scale. The response can then be averaged for each criterion and a score developed for the package.

It is best to have a two-stage decision for applications packages. That is, we divide the criteria for package selection into essential and nonessential groups. We can insist that, to be considered for acquisition, a package obtain a passing score on each essential criterion, which was established in advance. This procedure protects the information services department, which often has legitimate reasons for opposing a package. For example, reasons such as poor documentation or inability to understand and modify the code because of its lack of clarity are sufficient to warrant the rejection of a package.

If a package is acceptable and is the only alternative under consideration, we should acquire it. However, if several packages are available, then the ones that pass the screening test can be compared by ratings or scenarios describing processing under each option. If the package under consideration is an alternative to the development of an in-house system, the criteria established before the acquisition effort by a selection committee should be used to evaluate this package in comparison with other processing alternatives.

Expanding Role

Given the high cost of developing new applications, packaged programs are becoming increasingly important in the entire process for obtaining computer services. For some organizations, the presence of an adequate software package is even more important than the computer on which it runs. That is, when a firm acquires a turnkey system, it should be more concerned with how the package fits its needs than with the specific computer which executes the package.

Even for large organizations that do a substantial amount of custom programming with an internal staff, the availability of a package can make the difference in deciding what computer system to acquire. Over the past two decades, the emphasis in evaluation has shifted from the capabilities of the hardware to the ease of use and the power of software. It is expected that this trend will continue and that in the future more of the systems design effort will be devoted to comparing the functions of packaged software with the requirements of the organization.

CHAPTER 21

In Conclusion

IN THE PRECEDING CHAPTERS we discussed how management can cope more effectively with computing; I hope that we dispelled some of the mystique surrounding computers and the "foreign language" employed by computer specialists. Executives can now do more than cope with information processing; they can control it by following these essential guidelines:

Management must accept the ultimate responsibility for computing in the organization.

Top-level managers can easily understand enough to manage information processing, even given the high levels of technology involved.

The organization needs a plan for information systems in order to manage growth and evaluate progress.

Management should help set goals for information processing, be involved in major decisions about applications and in the systems design process, and provide resources to users and to the information services department.

Management needs an information services executive who is a manager and not a technician; this individual should be (1) treated as a manager and (2) made aware of the strategic plans of the firm.

Managers must be involved in:

The planning process for systems.
The identification of applications areas.
Systems-design decisions at the policy level.
The evaluation of applications development, operations, and the achievement of the targets in the information services plan.

By committing a modest effort to the understanding of information processing and by demonstrating a willingness to take action, management can control information processing instead of being controlled by it. No longer must the manager struggle with the computer; instead, information systems will make a major contribution to the daily operations of the firm and to corporate strategy. A management team that controls rather than copes with computing will enjoy the full potential of information processing and will have a major competitive advantage over other organizations.

Index